VIRTUAL REALITY

NEW EDITION

SCIENCE & TECHNOLOGY IN FOCUS

VIRTUAL REALITY

NEW EDITION

Simulating and Enhancing the World with Computers

Sean M. Grady

Facts On File, Inc.

Facts On File, Inc.
132 West 31st Street
New York NY 10001

Library of Congress Cataloging-in-Publication Data

Grady, Sean M., 1965–
Virtual reality : simulating and enhancing the world with computers /
Sean M. Grady.—New ed.
v. cm.—(Science and technology in focus)
Includes bibliographical references and index.
ISBN 0-8160-4686-7
1. Human-computer interaction—Juvenile literature. 2. Virtual
reality—Juvenile literature. [1. Human-computer interaction. 2. Virtual
reality. 3. Computer simulation.] I. Title. II. Series.
QA76.9.H85 G7195 2002
006—dc21   2002004380

Facts On File books are available at special discounts when purchased in bulk quantities for businesses, associations, institutions or sales, promotions. Please call our Special Sales Department in New York at 212/967-8800 or 800/322-8755.

You can find Facts On File on the World Wide Web at http://www.factsonfile.com

Text design by Erika K. Arroyo
Cover design by Nora Wertz
Illustrations by Sholto Ainslie © Facts On File, Inc.

Printed in the United States of America.

MP FOF 10 9 8 7 6 5 4 3 2 1

This book is printed on acid-free paper.

CONTENTS

ACKNOWLEDGMENTS

I wish to thank all those who provided their assistance as I researched and wrote this revised edition of *Virtual Reality*. In particular, I wish to thank:

Dr. Ulrich Neumann, director of the Integrated Media Systems Center at the University of Southern California; Dr. Tom Furness, director of the Human Interface Technology Lab at the University of Washington; Dace Campbell; John Bluck of NASA's Ames Research Center; Dr. Maxine Brown of the University of Chicago's Electronic Visualization Laboratory; Dr. John Bell of the University of Illinois at Chicago; Becky Underwood of Kelly Walsh High School, Casper, Wyoming; Dr. Donald H. Sanders of Learning Sites Inc.; Dawn Stage and Heather McBroom, Caterpillar Inc.; Bill Aulet of SensAble Technologies; Jared Baer of 5DT; Stephanie Lummis of antarcti.ca; Dr. Veronica Pantelidis of East Carolina University's Virtual Reality and Education Laboratory; Andrea Nolz and Walter Ratzat of Immersion Corporation; Ross R. Rainville of i-O Display Systems; Brian Donohue of VR Mariner; Virtually Better; Tim Gifford of VR Sim, Inc.; Marc Foglia of n-Vision Incorporated; and Frank Wodoslawsky of BTMD Inc.

I also wish to thank my editor, Frank K. Darmstadt, for his invaluable help and patience in the development of this project.

INTRODUCTION

Virtual reality, a term coined by computer programmer Jaron Lanier in 1988, has been used to describe a variety of methods for turning computers into something other than glorified typewriters. The phrase conjures up images of people plugging into their computers with display goggles and interactive controllers that allow them to experience and move within artificial environments in ways similar to—or utterly different than—those of the real world.

As Lanier originally meant it, and as many people understood it, the term *VR* is a shorthand way of referring to a combination of high-speed computers, advanced programming techniques, and interactive devices designed to make computer users feel they have stepped into another world—a world constructed of computer data. There even is a form of Web-based virtual reality that has been around, in one form or another, since the mid-1990s—VRML, the Virtual Reality Modeling Language that allows Web surfers to manipulate three-dimensional objects or move through on-screen worlds with mouse, trackball, or joystick. Over a brief time, though, other people began using the terms *virtual reality* and *VR* for just about every type of computerized presentation of data, including text-only multiple-user dungeons, or MUDS, and the chat rooms of the World Wide Web.

In "true" VR, users interact with digital domains in which data can appear in almost any form: a lamp that can be moved around a room; two molecules that can be combined to form a new drug; even a disembodied hand flying through an ocean of suspended bubbles. But virtual-reality systems do not depend on visual trickery alone. Some systems add sound to the images; for example, making the sound of a simulated fountain louder as the user "walks" toward it. In other systems, users control the simulations with electronic gloves that can provide the illusion of texture and solidity. All these sensations of vision, sound, and touch feed into the brain at once and help create the sense of a three-dimensional "reality." Presenting information as a virtual-reality construct makes manipulating data as easy as handling physical objects. By mimicking the way objects look and act in the physical world, virtual reality can help make computers more useful for the people who use them.

Virtual reality, of course, does not actually take anybody anywhere. VR users do not really merge with the world they perceive, nor do they somehow become part of the computer in the same way that a video monitor or a mouse does. However, the graphics displayed by VR systems are so realistic and the control tools are so easy to use that the user can easily think that he or she is in another world. That is the goal of virtual reality.

Although virtual reality is a technology of the computer age, its theoretical roots stretch back to discoveries about three-dimensional sight made in the early 1830s. Subsequent developments in photography, in the motion-picture industry, and in military technology also contributed to the history of VR. Rather than occurring as the result of a single inventor working toward a single goal, VR gradually came about from the independent work of many scientists, technicians, and designers.

Its inclusion in the real world of modern computing has been almost as gradual. In the five years after it was named, virtual reality became a media darling, as news reports and the entertainment industry presented the technology as the next exciting phase in the development of computing. Colleges around the world set up VR laboratories to figure out ways to use and improve the technology, and manufacturers set up shop to distribute and cash in on the hardware and software that seemed about to send the already booming information revolution to higher levels.

Then reality—real reality—set in. As with any technology in its infancy, virtual reality has posed tricky problems for its proponents to solve. Displaying virtual environments takes a lot of computing power—not only do computers have to draw and keep track of three-dimensional spaces and items, but they have to keep track of where users are within these worlds. The equipment that allows users to interact with these environments can be expensive, cumbersome, and—like other computer peripherals—quirky.

Even at its best, virtual reality does not provide the seamless, photographic presentation of cyberspace (a word created by science-fiction author William Gibson to describe a perceived world generated by computers) that is shown in such movies as *The Matrix*, *Virtuality*, or *Lawnmower Man*, all of which provided highly idealized, and cinematically enhanced, views of VR's capabilities. So, the mass public interest in virtual reality died down. Fortunately, the interest of researchers, designers, and other professionals did not, nor did the enthusiasm of students and fans of the technology. The tools of VR have been improved upon as computers have become more powerful, and VR is adapted to fields such as surgery, psychology, engineering, and meteorology, yielding results that many say could not have been attained without its help.

In architecture, VR techniques allow people to assemble, walk through, and redesign buildings before their real-world construction begins. VR design has already saved corporations millions of dollars that might have been spent on costly real-world modifications, and it has allowed collaboration on projects from municipal airports to football stadiums that could not have taken place otherwise.

In medicine, VR displays are being developed to teach anatomy without requiring students to dissect dead bodies and to help surgeons prepare to operate on patients, even those hundreds or thousands of miles away. Already, surgical researchers have been developing tools to give the surgeon a feel for how the operation is going while automated scalpels would do the actual work on the patient.

In the future, virtual reality may play the same role in everyday life that television, telephones, radios, and even the mail play today. Someday, as the state of technology advances, VR systems may be able to mimic the full range of textures, tastes, and scents of the physical world as well as its sights and sounds.

Virtual Reality: Simulating and Enhancing the World with Computers is a revised and expanded edition of *Virtual Reality: Computers Mimic the Physical World*, which was published in 1998 as part of the Science Sourcebooks series. The older book reflected the field of virtual reality at it was at the beginning of 1997. This new edition catches up with the developments that have taken place in the five years that followed, including the problems VR businesses encountered as a result of the technology boom-and-bust cycle that took place during the last few years of the twentieth century.

As in the earlier edition, this book will provide an overview of virtual-reality's history, the tools and techniques used to mimic the physical world, the fields in which VR is being used, and some of the obstacles that VR's supporters have had to overcome. Middle- and high-school students who already have taken part in immersive computing will find *Virtual Reality* a useful tool for learning how the technology came to be and where it might go in the future. For students who have not had any experience with virtual environments, this book will serve as a technological travel guide, pointing out some of the landmarks in this particular realm of computing. Technologies allied to VR, such as augmented reality and wearable computers, also will make an appearance, as will some of the philosophical issues raised by people outside and within the field who question the paths VR researchers have followed.

1

A QUICK TOUR OF VR

In 1966, Ivan Sutherland, a pioneer in the then-new field of computer graphics, began working on a device he had designed that would allow people to interact with computers in a unique way. The device, nicknamed the Sword of Damocles, hung from the ceiling on a pivoting metal post and sat like a helmet on a computer researcher's head. Using a set of glass prisms and two small video monitors, the mechanism reflected computer-generated images of objects such as wireframe boxes into the user's eyes. Each monitor displayed a slightly different image of the object; the brain combined these images into one seemingly three-dimensional form floating in midair.

Even more remarkably, the device—called a *head-mounted display*, or *HMD*—displayed different views of the three-dimensional object as the user's head moved. Sensors attached to the HMD constantly monitored which way the user was looking, allowing him to observe the object from many angles. As primitive and as cumbersome as it was (to wear the HMD, its users had to strap it on like a football helmet and stay within the reach of the support rod), Sutherland's device was the first major step toward the technology that would become virtual reality.

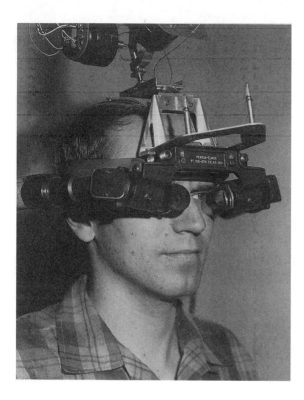

One of Ivan Sutherland's students tests out the Sword of Damocles head-mounted display Sutherland built in the 1960s. The two prisms in front of the student's eyes reflected computer images from the cylindrical cathode-ray tubes. (University of Utah/Evans & Sutherland Computer Corp.)

Until the late 1960s, most computers were chunky, gray behemoths that took up entire rooms; they were so expensive that only governments, universities, and large corporations could afford them. These computers were complicated machines to use. People programmed these computers using punched cards or punch tape—strips of thin cardboard or paper with patterns of holes that formed a code computers could read—or keyboards and switches that were part of a central control desk. Results usually were printed out on Teletypes or electric typewriters wired to the computer and sometimes were in a different code that only computer experts could decipher.

Adapting Computers to Users

Virtual reality came into being in the mid-to-late 1980s, following decades of research into ways to remove the hardware wall between computer users and computer data. With all the senses that human beings have, some computer researchers thought, why should people be limited to using mainly a keyboard, a video screen, and (starting in the 1980s) a mouse to handle data? Realizing there was no good answer to this question, the researchers began to develop computer systems that allowed people not just to process data but to play with it.

The computer scientists who set out to mimic the physical world soon realized that their goal would not be an easy one to reach. Tricking the brain into accepting a computerized world as real is a complicated process. Human beings experience the world in three dimensions: vertical (up and down), horizontal (left and right), and depth (near and far). The key to mimicking the physical world lies in replicating the third dimension, the one that conveys a sense of depth.

For the most part, three-dimensional, or 3-D, perception involves three of the five senses—vision, hearing, and touch. In humans, sight is the most heavily used sense, and it is the sense used most to perceive the 3-D world. People see in three dimensions using *binocular parallax.* Binocular means "two-eyed," and parallax refers to the way objects seem to change shape when viewed from different angles. Because the eyes are separated by about 6.5 centimeters, or a little over two and a half inches, each eye views the world at a slightly different angle from the other. These images overlap in the vision-processing area of the brain, which merges the signals coming from each eye into a single three-dimensional picture.

Hearing, the second-most heavily used sense people have, also gives people clues about the three-dimensional world. Upon hearing a noise, most people can tell from which direction it is coming and roughly judge the distance to its source. Indeed, some people who were born blind or who have lost their sight can navigate through a room by listening to the way sound echoes from objects around them. Many VR systems have achieved a great deal of success in mimicking the appearance of 3-D environments simply by combining audio and visual effects. Even some strictly two-dimensional multimedia systems—computers that contain compact disk (CD) players, sophisticated sound effect generators, and high-quality video monitors—are able to give users a feeling of being thrust into the third dimension.

The sense of touch backs up the sight-and-sound world picture with information about weight, shape, hardness, and other details that fix objects in all three dimensions. Touch-oriented, or *haptic,* devices—ones that vibrate, slow down, or otherwise convey a sense of how objects feel—are becoming a big part of many computer simulations.

They even play a role in non-VR computing, such as computer mice that provide touch effects when pointers glide over on-screen buttons or Internet links.

Smell and taste are far more difficult to simulate. Unlike the other three senses, smell and taste involve the analysis of chemicals that flow into the body from outside, a phenomenon that cannot be reproduced with clever electronic or mechanical tools. No chemicals, no odor; no chemicals, no flavor. Researchers have been experimenting with devices that can generate odors to accompany computer displays, and a few have been successful enough to make the leap from laboratory to the commercial market. Taste has posed an even greater problem, though, and is not likely to become a part of the human-computer interface anytime soon.

VR Basics

The systems that people use to enter *immersive environments*, the computer-generated 3-D worlds of VR, can be broken down into three parts. The centerpiece is a computer powerful enough to run the complex programs that simulate the real world and fast enough to avoid severe delays that interrupt the illusion of real-world action. Such a machine can be a home computer that is used for occasional forays into a simple 3-D action game, or it can be a *supercomputer* dedicated to maintaining high-level immersive environments. Whatever their form, these *reality simulators* require advanced *graphics boards*, compilations of *microprocessors* that create the three-dimensional images of the VR worlds; sound processors that can create 3-D sound effects to complement the images; and controllers for the various input and output devices that connect the computer user to the computer world.

These input/output accessories are known as *effectors*. They include head-mounted displays that transmit the reality simulator's 3-D images to the user (and, in some cases, transmit simulated 3-D sound as well) and *shutter glasses* that, combined with special display software, give the illusion of depth to two-dimensional video displays; *joysticks*, similar to those used in fighter jets, that are used to manipulate objects displayed in the HMD; *wired gloves* that track where the user's hands are and what he or she is doing; and other controls that translate human movement into movement of a computerized image in the computer's artificial world.

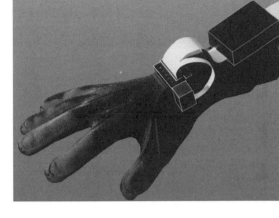

Some virtual-reality systems feature wired gloves like this one. Fiber-optic loops in the fingers and a motion-tracking sensor on top of the hand constantly monitor the user's actions, providing a real-time interface with the digital environment.
(Image courtesy: www.5dt.com)

The last part of any VR system is the computer user himself or herself, the person who controls what aspects of the virtual world the computer displays. To one degree or another, the user becomes a part of the computer, experiencing the illusion of directly controlling the environment, of having the computer respond to his or her gestures. Because VR offers a far more intimate way of interacting with computers than typing in keyboard commands or clicking mouse buttons, all the hardware components of VR attempt to adapt computers to their users.

A VR system can be nearly any size or shape. In the Cave Automatic Virtual Environment, or CAVE, three screens and four color projectors create three walls and the floor of a 10 × 10 × 10-foot cube in which people can share and interact with three-dimensional virtual worlds. With highly advanced versions of LCD (liquid-crystal display) shutter glasses, the CAVE can make virtual objects seem to float in a "real-world" space created upon the display screens. CAVE participants can easily manipulate objects or move around the environment using control wands linked to the computers generating the display. Another form of this display system uses a simplified version of CAVE technology to produce 3-D images on just one screen. This type of display was designed for office-oriented VR use, such as for architectural or mechanical design.

The main drawback to these projected VR systems is the amount of space they take up. Naturally, one could not stash a CAVE system, for example, in a corner of the family room. At the same time, these systems offer a type of effortless group interaction that is harder to achieve with HMD-and-glove systems.

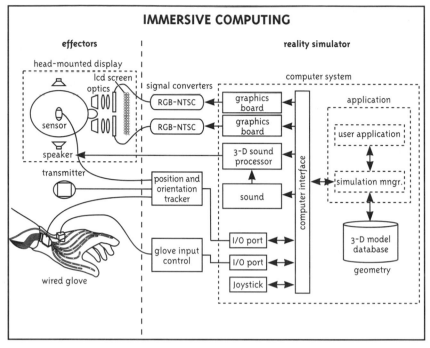

In general, virtual reality and other forms of immersive computing use computer systems similar to this one. The effectors are the tools that display the digital environment and allow users to interact with the system; the reality simulator is the computer and any intermediate devices that generate the environment.

Augmented Reality

Augmented reality is a related technology to virtual reality that uses many of the same tools as do VR systems. Augmented reality, or AR, differs from VR in that AR enhances, rather than replaces, one's view of the physical world. In a sense, AR is a return to the Sword of Damocles that Ivan Sutherland created in the 1960s. A typical augmented-reality system features transparent optics that reflect computer-generated images into the user's eye. This way, the images appear to overlay real objects in front of the user.

AR has the potential to become a real benefit to physicians, engineers, and other professionals who do intricate or complex tasks. Using an AR system, an airplane mechanic could project an instruction manual over his or her view of an airplane's engine, with arrows linking portions of diagrams to their real-world counterparts. Physicians could display *X-ray* or *ultrasound* images on their patients as they examined or operated on them. But these applications are a few years away. Right now, AR is in its developmental stage. A number of hurdles still must be overcome, the biggest of which is developing a way to make computers lay images precisely over real-world objects. If this and other problems are solved, mechanics might one day replace physical instruction manuals with a computer display built into a pair of glasses.

A third type of immersive-environment technology does not attempt to create the illusion of total immersion within the computerized environment. Instead, it combines video images of the user with computer graphics to create a system that responds to his or her actions. Called artificial reality, this method has been used in interactive sports games (such as a soccer game in which the player is a goalie trying to block video soccer balls) and in artistic displays.

Where the Virtual Worlds Are

For now, though—"now" being the beginning of the year 2002—much of the interaction between people and virtual displays takes place in university computer labs and corporate research centers. There are some notable exceptions, such as the virtual design offices of automobile makers such as Ford Motor Company, which uses an immersive computer system to craft the interiors of new car models. Such systems have been used for more than a decade: The construction equipment manufacturer Caterpillar used a CAVE-based system in the early 1990s to design an earth-moving machine that was easier to operate.

Some video games in arcades may be VR machines or use some VR gear. Home video-game consoles and personal-computer games have incorporated VR elements at various times, starting with a position-sensing glove built for the Nintendo Entertainment System in the late 1980s; recent accessories include the footstep-driven Power Pad. Personal video display goggles can provide images comparable to that of a 52-inch big-screen television.

For all the technology that has edged into the mainstream, though, VR itself is seen as a field that barely has been able to get off the ground. As recently as the year 2000, one of the first people to work in the realm of immersive computing—Dr. Fred Brooks, a University of North Carolina at Chapel Hill computer scientist—wrote an article in which he said that the technology of virtual reality "barely worked." By this, he meant that the equipment that brought users into computer environments had just about reached the point where it could mimic the physical world as well as its supporters hoped it would.

Of course, getting to that point took the last third of the 20th century and depended on the work of inventors dating back to the first half of the 19th century.

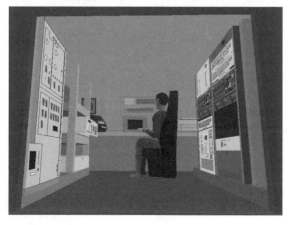

Nearly any type of instrument can be adapted to virtual reality. Here, computer-graphic reproductions of portable military communications equipment have been combined with human figures in a training system. [Image courtesy: VR Sim, Inc.]

2

CREATING PRACTICAL COMPUTERS

The story of how immersive devices and environments came to be begins with the invention of computers. These days, the word *computer* refers to a machine that contains microprocessor chips mounted on a series of circuit boards, together with input devices such as monitors, keyboards, mouse controllers, and other accessories. Even Internet servers, which send data around the world, and supercomputers, which handle the most complicated processing tasks, have components that are very similar to those in desktop computers.

In the past, though, the word *computer* was a job description. For at least 300 years—until the middle of the 20th century—computers were people who had good math skills and computed tables of figures for a living. This work could involve many simple calculations, like adding up a large company's sales sheets, or complicated work such as calculating star charts for astronomers.

Most of this work was tedious. All those calculations took a lot of time, and they all had to be double-checked by other human computers. Few tools were available to make the job easier. *Abaci* and *counting boards* helped speed up tasks that involved basic arithmetic, with stone, metal, or wood counters serving to keep track of a calculating job in progress. In the early 17th century, a Scottish mathematician named John Napier invented a device that made multiplication faster, using a series of four-sided, numbered rods that were fitted into a wooden frame. In effect, he sliced up the multiplication table and divided it among the rods. Depending on how the rods were lined up, the user could multiply or divide any two whole numbers.

A few other mathematicians built mechanical calculators in the 17th and 18th centuries, using gears to perform simple arithmetic. Unfortunately, these devices were fragile and difficult to use, breaking down as often as they yielded answers. They also were expensive to build, as their construction required the skills of a master craftsman, and few people could afford the cost.

Things were much different toward the end of the 19th century. The machinery created during the Industrial Revolution had reduced the cost and the time it took to make other machines, and people began to invent devices that they could not have made in earlier times. By 1890, people already were communicating by telephone in a few cities, stores were using cash registers to keep track of their sales, and office workers were using some of the first typewriters and calculators (which were mostly adding and subtracting machines) to speed up their work. This time was when the technology that led to computers began being developed.

Starting on the Path to Computers

One of the direct ancestors of the modern computer was a counting machine developed to speed up the United States census of 1890. The Constitution of the United States requires a census every 10 years to determine the number of representatives each state elects to Congress. When the U.S. Census Bureau started its work in 1790, counting heads and adding up the total by hand was easy, compared to doing the same task by hand today. There were only around 4,000,000 people in the 15 states that made up the nation back then, and arriving at a final population count took less than a couple of years. As the country and its population grew, the work took longer to complete, and the final count came out later and later.

The 1880 census was nearly a catastrophe. Counting every man, woman, and child in the United States, which took less than a year, was the easy part. Adding up the numbers—which included statistics on each person's age, sex, occupation, level of literacy, and other factors—took years. As early as 1881, the U.S. Census Bureau realized that the results would not be ready until nearly the end of the decade and would be badly out of date. The bureau also realized that, by the beginning of the 20th century, the results of one decade's census would not be ready until after the next decade's census had started.

The nation never reached that point, thanks to a Census Bureau agent and mechanical engineer named Herman Hollerith. Late in the summer of 1881, Hollerith and his supervisor were discussing the problem with the census and devising ways to speed up future head counts. Hollerith's supervisor mentioned that train tickets of the time served as passenger profile cards—with each passenger's features recorded using notches on the side of the ticket—and wished that the Census Bureau had a similar way to record information. Hollerith worked on this idea for the rest of the 1890s, creating a simple *tabulator* that used punched cards to record data and add up the results of the census. In doing so, he also created one of the first machines that allowed people to manipulate data using electricity.

A small, hand-operated press mounted on top of a narrow desk served as the card reader. The top of the press held hundreds of metal pins; the bottom held small cups filled with mercury, a metal that is liquid at room temperature. A panel of electric dial counters sat on the back of the desk, which was connected to an electrically operated sorting box with a wire cable. As a clerk closed the press over each card, some pins would pass through the holes in the card and dip into the mercury, completing an electric circuit. The dials on top of the desk were wired into those circuits; closing a circuit would advance the matching dials one position and pop open a lid on one of the slots in the sorting box. All the clerk who was running the cards through the machine had to do was insert the card in the reader, press down the reader's handle, and put the card in the open slot.

In July 1890, Census Bureau clerks began entering the data from the 1890 census on punched cards and running them through 56 Hollerith tabulators that the bureau purchased, as well as a special-purpose machine Hollerith built to calculate the total figure for the U.S. population. Six weeks after the clerks started their work, they knew that there were 62,622,250 people living in the nation. Better still, it took less than seven years to calculate the population of each state and issue tables of the other statistical information the census had been designed to collect.

News of the amazing tabulators spread across the world, and Hollerith—who had started a business, the Tabulating Machine Company, to capitalize on his invention—soon began receiving orders. Foreign governments needed the tabulators for their own census work, and large companies realized they could adapt the machines to provide

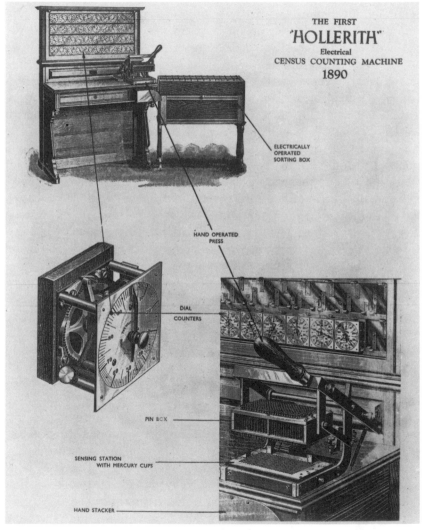

THE FIRST
"HOLLERITH"
Electrical
CENSUS COUNTING MACHINE
1890

ELECTRICALLY
OPERATED
SORTING BOX

HAND OPERATED
PRESS

DIAL
COUNTERS

PIN BOX

SENSING STATION
WITH MERCURY CUPS

HAND STACKER

Herman Hollerith's census tabulating machine is one of the direct mechanical ancestors of today's computers. [Courtesy IBM Archives]

much-needed assistance in their inventory and accounting departments. Over the next few decades, punched-card tabulators and calculators from Hollerith's firm (which merged with a couple of other companies and eventually became International Business Machines [IBM]) and a few other companies became mandatory office equipment for large firms that wished to succeed in business.

Faster Calculators for Science

For scientific uses, though, tabulators and calculators were inconvenient. Even after the introduction of electric motors, the machines were too slow and technologically unsophisticated for most science research and engineering projects. A few punched-card systems were set up to run batches of instructions over and over again to calculate simple math tables, such as the position of the Moon as it orbited the Earth over a handful of decades. But this method could not be used to solve the equations involved in analyzing how friction, gravity, and other forces influence moving objects, such as airplanes and artillery shells, and affect stationary objects, such as bridges. These forces can work with or against one another, and their effects can grow or decrease in strength. To account for these variable conditions, scientists and engineers rely on calculations called differential equations, which are very difficult to solve. For decades, only a human being, with the assistance of an electric desktop calculator, could do that type of math.

Then, in the 1930s, two university researchers devised machines that resolved part of the problem. At the Massachusetts Institute of Technology (MIT) in the middle of the decade, an engineering professor named Vannevar Bush built an electrically powered mechanical calculator called the differential analyzer, which used gear wheels and spinning metal shafts to solve differential equations. With changes in the arrangement of the gears and gear shafts, Bush's device could analyze a wide range of engineering and scientific phenomena. It was not a perfect solution; technicians had to spend days changing gears for each job, and one or two people constantly had to make small adjustments to the mechanism while it was working. But, for a few years, the differential analyzer was the most advanced calculating machine in the world.

Near the end of the decade, a graduate student at Harvard University, Howard Aiken, thought of a way to use punched-card tabulators and sorters in a machine that would go beyond the abilities of the differential analyzer. The Automatic Sequence Controlled Calculator (ASCC), built by IBM, performed its mathematical duties using a 51-foot-long sequence of 3,300 electric-powered mechanical relays. Programming the five-ton ASCC involved setting about 1,400 switches and feeding in long loops of punch-tape instructions; the machine printed out its answers on punched cards and a series of electric typewriters. The ASCC—also called the Harvard Mark I, because it was used almost exclusively at the university—was a powerful machine for its time; during a demonstration, it took only three seconds to multiply two numbers in the tens of sextillions (a sextillion is the number one followed by 21 zeroes).

IBM installed the machine at Harvard in 1944, during World War II, where it spent the final year of the war calculating firing tables for the United States Navy. Firing tables are books showing how the trajectories of naval guns and land-based artillery change based on weather conditions, geography, and other variable conditions. The equations that revealed these facts were differential equations, and, until the 1940s, the armed forces of every major military power employed hundreds of human computers to run through these calculations by hand. This work was vital, because gun crews could waste dozens of shells trying to zero in on a target without having a firing table to give them at least an initial trajectory. However, it took months to prepare a set of tables for each type of gun, and during wartime, the work almost always fell behind the need.

Just as the navy leased the Mark I when it heard of the machine's construction, the United States Army invested in another giant calculator to solve its artillery table problems. Shortly before the United States entered World War II, two engineers from the University of Pennsylvania's Moore School of Engineering, John Mauchly and J. Presper Eckert, had designed a huge electronic calculator to replace the differential analyzer and its dependence on gears and camshafts. Their machine solved equations using thousands of *vacuum tubes*—glass tubes that look like long, clear light bulbs with a few rows of wire filaments—mounted in rows on large circuit boards. The vacuum tubes Mauchly and Eckert used were the electronic equivalent of light switches, with a high-power "on" setting and a low-power "off" state. Each circuit board could store a single number from one to nine, and separate circuit boards stored different categories of numbers: units, tens, hundreds, thousands, and so forth.

When Mauchly and Eckert proposed building their machine for the army in early 1943—they had tried but failed to get a grant to build the machine a few years before—the army saw it as a way to produce firing tables faster. The two scientists had designed their machine—called the Electronic Numerical Integrator and Calculator, or ENIAC—to solve a range of complex equations as well as handle simple arithmetic, and it seemed ideally suited for the task of calculating trajectories. The army paid the Pennsylvania researchers to build ENIAC, hoping it would be ready before the end of the war.

Unfortunately, it wasn't. The team Mauchly and Eckert assembled took more than two and a half years to get ENIAC ready to work. When unveiled in 1946, however, ENIAC proved that electronic systems could calculate not just faster than human computers but faster than any electromechanical device like the Mark I. Calculating the trajectory of an artillery shell took ENIAC 20 seconds, 10 seconds less than it took a shell to reach its target. A reporter covering a public demonstration of the machine said it worked "faster than thought" when he saw it multiply a five-digit number by itself 5,000 times in less than half a second.

What the reporter did not see was the amount of time it took to get ENIAC ready for its task. It took technicians the better part of two full days to program ENIAC to solve an equation, setting thousands of switches and connecting the hundreds of wire cables that allowed the more than 40 circuit-filled cabinets and other components of ENIAC to talk to one another. Then a set of punched cards containing the initial data had to be entered into the reader. When ENIAC finished its work, it printed the results on another set of cards that were deciphered on a separate machine. And when tubes burned out, the computer could not be used until troubleshooters located and replaced them, a task that was both costly and time consuming.

New Designs for Computers

To many historians, the creation of ENIAC marks the beginning of the computer age, the point at which people began calculating using electrons rather than gear wheels. At the time, however, Mauchly and Eckert knew that the words of praise from the press were a bit more than ENIAC deserved, considering its limitations, the biggest one being the fact that it could not store a program for later use. Each calculation run was a custom job. By the time ENIAC was switched on, though, the two engineers had come up with a design for its successor, one that solved most of the problems with ENIAC's design and used far fewer vacuum tubes and other components. Once again, the army approved the construction of a Mauchly/Eckert math machine: This one was the Electronic Discrete Variable Calculator, or EDVAC.

The design of EDVAC marked the first use of the stored-program concept in electronic computing. A stored-program computer is one in which the instructions that tell the machine what to do are loaded directly into its memory. Unlike ENIAC, which had to be rewired for each type of calculation, a stored-program computer never needs to have its circuits changed. Mauchly and Eckert realized that this way of building computers would make EDVAC faster than ENIAC, as EDVAC would take less time to program and would be able to act on its instructions more rapidly.

EDVAC was switched on in 1952, but it was not the first stored-program computer. In 1948 and 1949, two groups of British scientists who had read about EDVAC's design assembled similar computers, proving that the general design could work while adding a few improvements of their own. These and other machines built in the 1950s generally used vacuum tubes in their processing circuitry, though engineers soon devised ways to store data temporarily in magnet-based memory circuits and permanently on magnetic tape and other materials.

Still, using vacuum tubes to control the flow of electricity through computers was a problem. Even the smallest tubes took up a lot of space and generated a lot of heat, forcing computer manufacturers to build room-size systems equipped with power-hungry fans to cool themselves down. A burned-out tube could shut down an entire room full of equipment in an instant. And the cost of maintaining and replacing tube-based computers easily totaled tens of thousands of dollars (hundreds of thousands in today's money).

These problems vanished by the early 1960s, when *transistors* replaced vacuum tubes in the circuits of new computers, as well as other devices such as radios and televisions. Transistors are made of small, solid blocks of materials called semiconductors; electricity flows through transistors at varying rates, depending on the chemical makeup of the semiconductor material. Three researchers at Bell Laboratories—William Shockley, Walter Brattain, and John Bardeen—created the first crude transistors in 1948 specifically to replace vacuum tubes in electronic circuitry, but the devices were too expensive to produce until nearly a decade after their invention. Once the cost came down, computer manufacturers and users alike were eager to use transistors, which were smaller than vacuum tubes, used far less energy, and were less vulnerable to damage.

Even with the adoption of transistors, working with the thinking machines was time-consuming, complicated, and somewhat mystical to all but those who actually told computers what to do. Making computers that were easier to use was not a priority. Computer companies did not even offer to program the machines they built and serviced; that task was the customer's responsibility. Of course, in the 1950s, nobody thought that there would be more than a few hundred computers in the world, given the size and the cost of the gigantic machines. And nobody really thought that the public would ever use computers.

As a result, computers were extremely user-unfriendly. Programming a computer or entering data for it to work on—such as corporate accounting sheets or temperature and air pressure readings for weather forecasts—often required technicians to prepare hundreds of punched cards to feed in data. Some computers presented their results on other sets of punched cards that had to be run through a separate printing system. Other computers printed out their results in a code that only programmers could read. And when computers were designed to yield answers in plain English, the answers usually came out on a Teletype or an electric typewriter, slowing down the interaction between human and machine even more.

Computers had become a fixture of the modern world. It would take a lot of work, though, to make them part of everyday life.

3

DEVELOPING BETTER INTERFACES

Around the time that transistors began to replace vacuum tubes, a few computer scientists were trying to change the way people interacted with computers. These researchers thought that computers could be used for more tasks than simply handling business accounts, predicting the weather, or generating firing tables for the military. Their desire was to turn computers into all-purpose information machines that could help people with their daily work and, maybe, help solve the increasingly complex problems of life in the fast-growing modern world.

One of the first people to think about using computers this way was an engineer named Douglas Engelbart. During World War II, Engelbart had been exposed to the basics of electronics while he served as a radar technician in the United States Navy. He put his skills to work after the war, first by earning a degree in electrical engineering and then by joining a northern California electronics firm that was developing improved radar displays. In 1950, Engelbart's interests switched to the new field of computing. Radar systems and computers, he realized, did very similar things. Both devices translated electronic signals into a form that human beings could use. The difference was that radar screens showed the position of moving objects on a view screen, while computers at that time showed the results of electronic calculations on paper printouts.

This realization led Engelbart to start planning a system that combined the computer's information-processing abilities with a television-style display. The first designs he sketched out for this hybrid computer had it displaying reports, graphs, and other information on-screen, with a selection of knobs and levers people could use to change their view from one document or display to another. Engelbart knew virtually nothing about the state of computer technology at the time, aside from articles he had read, but he believed that the newborn computer industry at least could begin to explore his idea to create problem-solving machines for nonprogrammers.

Engelbart left his job at the electronics firm to learn more about how computers were being put together and to find some place where he could improve his design. He soon discovered that no one, either in the electronics industry or the academic world, was willing to spend money right then on developing a machine that people could use to solve nonmathematical problems. Just the idea of using a video screen to create and display images was enough to turn away potential supporters. It was hard enough, people said, to get computers to do the work they were designed to perform without trying to add to their burden. Engelbart ended up going to work at the Stanford Research Institute, a special technology development center set up by Stanford University in Palo Alto, California. There, he learned more about how computers were being developed while he refined his ideas for his improved way of using these thinking machines.

A SAGE Approach to National Defense

As it turned out, researchers already had developed a computer system that came close to doing what Engelbart wanted his machine to do—he just had not known about it. The computer was the main component of a project to protect the continental United States from a bomber or missile attack during the cold war with the Soviet Union. Called the Semi-Automatic Ground Environment, or SAGE, the system came into being at the Lincoln Laboratory, a computer research center that the Massachusetts Institute of Technology established in the early 1950s specifically to design and build the system. (The acronym SAGE also was a play on words: A sage is a wise person who can calmly analyze and respond to situations.)

SAGE tied a network of radar stations into a series of computers that identified potentially hostile aircraft. The computer also helped military personnel guide fighter-interceptor airplanes toward these targets to see if they were truly threats or not. The SAGE computers displayed information using very simple dots and line drawings on circular video screens, along with letter-and-number, or *alphanumeric*, codes to identify these dots as friendly craft or as intruders.

SAGE's display was primitive compared to the displays available today, but it marked three major advances in how people interacted with computers. First, its creators devised this method of displaying information in the early 1950s, when computer graphics generally meant using a computer to plot mathematical designs on a sheet of paper. Second, the computer generated and displayed these images in what came to be called "real time"—in other words, the computer displayed the information gathered by its radar stations as fast as it received the signals, with nearly no delay in processing time. It accomplished this feat thanks to a very fast type of memory circuit that used small magnets to store information, and signals from electric wires to place data on these magnets and read from them. There still were vacuum tubes in the SAGE computers, but they were fast enough not to interfere with the speed of the display.

The third remarkable thing about the SAGE display was that it used simple push buttons, joysticks, and an input device called a *light pen* to receive its instructions from its human operators. People found that the light pen—versions of which are used today—was especially useful in picking out details on the screen. Cathode-ray tubes (CRT), including television picture tubes, contain electron-beam generators that paint a line of electrons on the inside of the tube's screen. The screen's inner surface is coated with chemicals called phosphors that light up and slowly dim when the electrons hit them. The beam scans across and down the picture screen so fast that people usually cannot sense when the phosphors are fading, but light pens are sensitive enough to pick up the flash of the phosphors as the beam refreshes the picture. A signal from the pen to the circuitry controlling the electron beam tells the computer where the pen is pointing on the screen. Using the pen, SAGE's operators could select single targets or groups of targets for constant identification.

Sketching the Future of Computing

By the late 1950s, SAGE was ready for duty, and the Lincoln Laboratory researchers turned the design over to IBM, which the government had chosen to build the computer systems for 23 command stations across the nation. MIT kept the laboratory open to work on other government computing projects and to push the technology into new areas. One of the researchers who came to the laboratory over the next few years was a graduate student named Ivan Sutherland. Like Engelbart, Sutherland wanted to create a simplified way for anyone, not just those with special training, to use computers. He focused on improved computer graphics as the method to make this happen.

Though on-screen computer graphics still were crude and experimental, researchers were getting their machines to do some amazing feats that showed how future computers might be used. For example, four other graduate students studying elsewhere at MIT created a popular computer video game, Spacewar, that they played on a computer with a circular video screen. Using handmade control boxes, players flew tiny spaceships around the screen, which displayed a star field and a sun in the center of the screen. The goal was to blow up the opponent's spaceship while avoiding a collision with the sun.

In 1962, Sutherland took the level of interaction between human and machine one step closer with his work at the laboratory. The computer he worked with was an early transistor-based machine, the TX-2, which had a nine-inch monitor. He created a program that turned a keyboard and a light pen into tools people could use to draw shapes and figures on the screen. Touching the pen to the screen started a line that could be drawn in any direction and for almost any length desired. By typing in the right instructions, users could attach lines to one another, change the angles between two lines, and perform other artistic tricks. The program, which Sutherland named Sketchpad, also allowed users to save their work for later modification, copy the designs they drew, and enlarge or reduce the pictures on screen. At a time when the only way to copy an image quickly was to use a photocopier, and making images larger or smaller generally required a photo lab, Sketchpad was revolutionary.

As it turned out, Sutherland developed Sketchpad at just the right time. The cold war between the United States and the Soviet Union had developed into a competition of high technology; Soviet satellites had been orbiting Earth starting in 1957, and a Soviet cosmonaut, Yuri Gagarin, rocketed into orbit in 1961. As part of the race to close this technology gap, the federal government established a special research and development group within the Department of Defense, the Advanced Research Project Agency (ARPA), and ordered it to support as many cutting-edge projects as it could.

In 1962, ARPA selected an MIT researcher, J. C. R. Licklider, to establish and run a program called the Information Processing Techniques Office (IPTO), which would sponsor projects to create and improve military computer systems at a few universities around the nation. ARPA's chiefs decided that Licklider would be perfect for the job partly because of a paper he wrote in 1960 called "Man-Computer Symbiosis" that set a goal for computer development, which researchers would spend the next few decades trying to reach.

People spend most of their time getting set up to do things, and fairly little time actually doing them, Licklider wrote in his paper. He used his own work as an example: In order to solve a particularly tricky scientific problem, Licklider had to spend hours tracking down information and drawing graphs to compare the results of various experiments. After spending hours finishing this preliminary work, he took only a handful of seconds to decide what to do with the information he had gathered. If computers could speed up the time it took to gather and analyze information, Licklider concluded, people could spend more time on the important aspects of their work. He used the word *symbiosis*, which means a beneficial relationship, to describe how valuable computers could be to people who were not scientists, business executives, or military personnel.

With IPTO under his command, Licklider began supporting researchers who seemed to be working on this type of machine. Two groups of researchers in particular, one at the Lincoln Laboratory and another at the University of Utah, had been trying to improve the quality of computer graphics, but they had been having a hard time figuring out how people would control on-screen information. During a meeting on how to solve this problem, Licklider asked Sutherland to give a slide presentation of his work on Sketchpad. This was a big step for Sutherland; he had not yet earned his doctorate, and he was being asked to present his work to a roomful of experienced scientists. However, Licklider and the others knew Sutherland was working on an advanced graphics program of his own, and they thought it would be worthwhile to hear what he had to say.

The presentation was more than worthwhile; in later years, the people who attended the slide show and saw Sketchpad in action described the experience as a "revelation." With Sketchpad, Sutherland had done far more than any of the more-experienced scientists had thought could be done at the time. In fact, many historians and computer experts say that Sketchpad's development marks the beginning of modern computer graphics. Without a doubt, the field of computer-assisted design—in which people use advanced computers to design houses, cars, and other objects on-screen—is tied directly to the innovative use of computers that Sketchpad represents. Finally, Sutherland not only earned his doctorate with Sketchpad, but he impressed Licklider enough for the older scientist to recommend him as the new head of IPTO in 1964.

Building a New Form of Computing

Sketchpad's invention was a major event in the history of modern computing, but it did not have much of an effect outside the world of cutting-edge computer research in the early 1960s. For one thing, the TX-2 was one of the few computers powerful enough to run the program, and few institutions could afford a machine of its abilities. Aside from the cost of the hardware, the Sketchpad program was little more than a means of proving Sutherland's theories of how computer graphics could be manipulated. It was a good tool for further exploration of computer graphics; it was not something that was ready for use in the real world.

Many inventions, and whole fields of technology, go through similar stages of development. People often do not benefit from important breakthroughs until years or decades afterward, when the original device had been developed into a practical, usable form. Many of these kinds of breakthroughs in computer technology happened during the 1960s, when devices that people now take for granted were new.

Douglas Engelbart helped create another one of these technological breakthroughs that immediately inspired computer scientists but took longer to reach the public. In his spare time while he worked at the Stanford Research Institute, and later for a private computer company, Engelbart continued refining his plans for a computer that would enhance the work of the people who used it. When the Information Processing Techniques Office opened for business in 1962, he was one of the first researchers to apply for funds. And just as Licklider's work had impressed the ARPA executives who hired him, Engelbart's work on computers that could benefit humans—along with the recommendation of a supervisor—earned him Licklider's interest and support.

Engelbart's ideas, which he published in a series of articles, sounded as though he was describing today's computers, and some VR systems, at work. In one paper, he suggested that a future architect might use a computer-assisted drawing table to design houses. Instead of a standard drafting board, which is about three feet on a side, Engelbart imagined a board-shaped computer-graphics display screen that was wired to a computer. The architect would control the display using a small keyboard and a sort of pointing device to draw lines and select features within the design. The screen could start with a display of the lot on which a house would be built; using the pointer and keyboard, the architect would excavate a space for the foundation, add walls and a roof, and draw in the rest of the exterior.

If the computer contained data about building materials, interior hardware, fixtures, and furniture, the architect could design the entire house on the drafting table's screen. Better still, Engelbart thought, the architect could use the computer to calculate how the design would stand up to the elements over time, how well people could move through the house, and even if reflected sunlight from any windows could blind passing drivers. Engelbart concluded this image of computer augmentation at work by pointing out that this system could make it easier for people to collaborate on projects. Other architects, builders, and the house's owner could review and alter the house plans simply by loading a tape of the digital "design manual" into their own computers.

This example, and others that Engelbart suggested, seem to have predicted how people would be using computers in the coming decades. Certainly, the idea of using computers as architectural tools has proved accurate. Many large architectural firms have been using such systems for years, and home-design and landscaping programs that include three-dimensional *visualization* techniques are available for personal computers.

An Easier Human-Computer Interface

With IPTO's support, Engelbart started a special research group in 1963 to create machines that might lead to his goal of augmenting human work. Over the next five years in their lab at the Stanford Research Institute, this group developed a working model of an office computer that could do away with typewriters, copying machines, and paper documents altogether. The researchers unveiled the result of their work, the On-Line System, during a 1968 computer science conference in San Francisco. Engelbart sat on stage with the machine, demonstrating the computer and explaining how the new technology worked as an overhead movie screen displayed live images of what he was doing.

While his audience watched, Engelbart used a box-shaped pointing device connected to the computer with a wire cable to move a cursor on the computer screen. The pointer, which Engelbart explained was called a *mouse*, rolled on two wheels that controlled the cursor's horizontal and vertical movement. With the mouse, he opened documents in the computer's memory, displaying them in text windows. He selected words within the documents and moved them around the screen, changing their position within a sentence or simply deleting them. He even showed how the system could manipulate pictures as well as words.

These feats might not seem that remarkable to modern-day computer users, but for 1968, they were nothing less than amazing. Like Sketchpad, the On-Line System was too expensive and experimental for widespread use. However, the fact that it worked and the things it could do opened up the minds of the people who saw it, as well as the people who built it, to new possibilities of research and development. By showing how simple it could be to create and manipulate information in a computer, the On-Line System, like Sketchpad before it, spurred on the development of better interfaces, including the tools of immersive computing.

PRECURSORS TO VR

The idea of creating a pseudo-reality within a small space is not new. People have been mimicking the effects of the real world for thousands of years in works of art such as paintings and more recently in photographs, movies, and other media. During the height of the Roman Empire, wealthy homeowners painted the inner walls of their city dwellings with realistic scenes of orchards and gardens. These designs often presented a view of a marble porch leading away from the hall or room into a sunny countryside. Because things that are far away look smaller than they do close-up, the artists who painted these wall-sized images combined large and small images with other artistic techniques to give the illusion of depth. These methods drew the viewer's eye into the painting, making it seem as if there really was another landscape leading away into the distance.

Artists in many nations developed similar styles of painting or drawing to give a sense of perspective to their artwork—a sense of perspective that was highly limited, that is. No matter how well they were made, the paintings and drawings did not have any true depth. They remained two-dimensional representations of a three-dimensional world, just as photographs can only capture a flat image of a scene or a subject. In the early 19th century, artists began working around this limitation to immersion by creating dioramas, artworks that arranged sculpted figures and other objects in front of a realistically painted background. Some of these pieces were so well arranged that, at first, people could not tell where the painting stopped and the physical objects began.

Reality to Go

Other people searched for less-bulky ways to re-create the sense of depth in artwork. In 1833, a British physicist and inventor named Sir Charles Wheatstone created a parlor toy he called a *stereoscope*. Wheatstone had been experimenting with the phenomenon of binocular parallax, the way that the brain combines the two slightly different views of the world it gets from the eyes to create the sense of stereoscopic vision. Wheatstone's stereoscope was a simple wooden framework that a person could hold in front of his or her face, using a handle attached to the bottom of the frame. A slot on each side of the viewer's head held one of two cards that showed a slightly different view of the same drawing. Two small mirrors angling out from the viewer's nose reflected the cards' images into the viewer's eyes.

As the brain merged the two images into one, the viewer suddenly saw the drawing spring to life—not moving, but seeming to pop into three dimensions. Sir David Brewster, another British inventor, improved upon Wheatstone's device in 1844. Brewster put both views on the same card and mounted the card on a moveable slide that helped focus the image in front of the viewer's face. He also placed a half lens in front of each eye to make sure the images would properly blend. By sliding the card toward and away from the eyes, each viewer could position it at the distance that gave him or her the best 3-D illusion.

This type of stereoscope became immensely popular around the world in the last half of the 19th century and the first few decades of the 20th. As cameras became more sophisticated and less expensive, photographs replaced drawn or painted illustrations. The companies that made stereoscopic images created the illusion of three-dimensional images with a simple trick. A photographer would set up his camera on a special tripod, which had a rail that allowed the camera to move sideways a few inches, roughly the distance between most people's eyes. The photographer would take one picture, move the camera sideways, and take the second picture.

Stereoscopes were entertaining, giving people a view of places they could not visit or places they had been to and wanted to remember in greater detail than a plain photograph could provide. The viewers also were destined to have a long life in the form of the ViewMaster, a binocular-shaped stereoscopic viewer that uses tiny photographic slides mounted on cardboard circles. While it gave visual depth, though, the stereoscope offered little else in the way of reproducing reality. The images did not move and there was no sound (aside from a few viewers in later years that contained tape recorders or other playback machines). Adding these details would take the efforts of a more complex entertainment industry.

Immersing the Audience

For as long as movies have been around, motion-picture companies have sought ways to make moviegoers feel as if they were inside the movies, not just watching them. When the first motion pictures were presented to the public in the 1890s and early 1900s, the illusion of immersion was hard to attain. Early movies were of poor quality compared to those of today. The pictures were black-and-white and grainy, had no sound, and were beamed by noisy projectors onto screens the size of a bed sheet. The audiences of the time were not very sophisticated, though. Some customers ran screaming from the theater, afraid of being run over by oncoming horsemen or being shot by bandits whose revolvers seemed to be aimed right at them.

Sound came to the movies in the 1920s, adding to their realism. Soon after, elaborate special effects heightened the impact of many movies, from war stories to horror films, bringing the audience even further into the picture. Then, after World War II, the sudden mass appeal of television began drawing audiences away from the theaters. Moviemakers tried a number of gimmicks to keep attendance levels up, including one method that brought the third dimension of depth onto the flat surface of the movie screen.

The 3-D experiment was one of the most innovative gambles in the history of motion pictures, primarily because moviemakers could only make films using two-dimensional footage. Fortunately, the illusion of 3-D could be created with a two-dimensional film since light waves vibrate in many different directions. The direction in which a beam of light vibrates is called its *polarity*. Sunlight and the light from lightbulbs vibrate in many directions at once—left and right, up and down, diagonally, and so forth. Special filters called *polarizers* pass light rays of one polarity and block all others.

Using polarizers and a few other devices attached to their cameras, filmmakers recorded two different polarities of each scene onto the same film. While watching the finished movie, audiences wore special glasses that had separately polarized lenses over each eye. Each eye saw only one polarity of the movie; the brain blended the two images, creating the 3-D effect.

A noble experiment, 3-D was too expensive (and many 3-D movies were too poorly made) for the technique to last. Although a few companies made attempts to bring it back over the next three decades, 3-D as a cinematic experience essentially died out in the mid-1950s. Ironically, though, it was an innovative Hollywood filmmaker in the 1950s who came closest to creating what might have been the first stage of virtual reality.

Entertaining the Senses

Morton Heilig started working on movies in the early 1950s, around the beginning of the motion-picture industry's fling with Cinerama. Cinerama was an extreme wide-angle filming technique that employed three cameras to shoot each scene and three projectors to show the movie on a huge curved movie screen. Enthralled with the way Cinerama seemed to surround the audience with the movie, Heilig had an idea of creating an even more personal experience. He wanted to engage all the senses, to entertain the audience with the feel and smell of the story as well as with the story's sights and sounds. He first attempted to find a way to present these physical sensations to large movie theater audiences, but soon realized that the expense involved made this grand scheme impracticable. He then concentrated on immersing just one person in an all-encompassing display as a means both of demonstrating his idea and of earning enough money to develop it further.

By 1960, after six years of work, Heilig had developed two separate devices for presenting three-dimensional simulations of reality. One device, which he patented in 1960, was like the old stereoscopic viewers of the late 19th and early 20th centuries. It combined a three-dimensional slide viewer with stereo headphones and a perfume spray to entertain users with synchronized sights, sounds, and smells. Moreover, this display was portable—Heilig designed it like a mask, with a brace that went around the user's head. Heilig envisioned replacing the slide viewer with tiny TV screens once technological advances made the substitution possible, creating a three-dimensional, head-mounted TV set.

Unfortunately, while Heilig's prototypical head-mounted display was unique—it earned its inventor a U.S. patent—it did not capture the interest of either the television or the motion-picture industries. No one would pay to develop the device, and Heilig had to give up any further work on it. In addition to his personal viewer design, however, Heilig had put together a one-person arcade ride called the Sensorama. The ride featured a plastic bucket seat mounted in front of a periscope-like display that contained a small 3-D movie screen, stereo speakers, fans, and, as in his stereo headset, a device for reproducing odors. The Sensorama featured a number of scenarios, including a motorcycle ride through New York City. This part of the display came complete with the sensations of bouncing over potholes, hearing traffic pass by on each side, feeling the wind against the rider's face, and smelling food from restaurants.

Like the personal viewer, Sensorama was not destined to be part of the modern world. Heilig sold a few of these machines, but they proved unable to withstand the stress of daily arcade use. Breakdowns were frequent, and the arcade owners who purchased these troublesome machines eventually unplugged them and removed them from their amusement centers. Sensorama had another, even more serious, drawback: The experience it offered was passive, like an enhanced television show. Sensorama users were simply along for the ride, unable to interact with or have any effect on the display. Once the ride was over, there was nothing left to entice a customer to try it again. Unable to interest anyone in the entertainment industry in helping him improve his machine, Heilig eventually had to shelve his dreams of an all-encompassing movie.

Morton Heilig's head-mounted television display and Sensorama turned out to be classic examples of ideas that came before their time. Even though the ideas were revolutionary, the revolution they promised was apparent to few people aside from their creator. Moviemakers concentrated on techniques that made 2-D films seem larger than life, later adding advanced sound-recording methods that improved the quality of movie sound. For the most part, the entertainment industry gave up on trying to cross the boundary between two-dimensional displays and the three-dimensional world. But over the next few decades, the knowledge about how to trick people into seeing 3-D images on 2-D screens would come in handy to scientists working in the computer industry.

Simulating Flight

In one way, Sensorama was behind the times. Machines that simulated moving vehicles had been available for decades when Heilig's first motorcycle ride went into operation; they allowed their occupants to control their direction of travel, and they presented challenging situations that had to be handled as though they were happening in real life. The only catch was that to use these simulators, the occupants had to join the military.

In 1929, a company that made player pianos and pipe organs, the Link Corporation, developed a training tool that helped student pilots learn the basic skills of flying. The simulator was a realistic mock-up of an airplane cockpit mounted on a platform that tilted in response to the actions of the "pilot." The head of the Link Corporation, Edwin Link, was a fan of aviation, which was only in its third decade of existence. At first, Link had wanted to create a carnival ride for people who were too poor or too timid to attempt flight in a real airplane. But Link's flight simulator was so well crafted that it soon found a place in the professional flying world.

The Link Trainer found enthusiastic customers in the United States Army Air Corps (the predecessor to the United States Air Force) and in the United States Navy's aviation division. The great air battles of World War I had provided one crucial bit of knowledge for fighter pilots—if a pilot survived his first five dogfights, he reasonably could expect to survive a war. The problem was that, during the war, many pilots got into their first dogfights while they still were getting accustomed to how their aircraft worked and figuring out how to keep it in the sky. The military realized that by using simulators, flight instructors could speed up the time it took for pilots to get used to their planes. That way, their students could use more of their real flight time practicing combat maneuvers. This knowledge, in turn, would give many pilots the edge they needed to live through their initial dogfights.

Training new pilots after the war was an equally tricky matter. Until the Link Trainer became available, there was no way to prepare the trainees for the sensation of flight or to give them a feel for how their planes would respond until they were in the air with an instructor. Student and teacher both were at risk of accidental stalling or other mishaps while the student tried to apply his book learning to the actual experience. With a simulator, new pilots could prepare themselves at least to a small degree for what awaited them in the air.

The first few generations of flight simulators recreated the basic aspects of flight, allowing students to learn the mechanics of how the various controls worked and to experience the general effect they had on the airplane. Students had to wait until they were actually flying through clouds or over hostile terrain to get accustomed to those situations. Later, other companies developed advanced simulators that produced a more accurate simulation. For example, during World War II, films taken from the windows of real airplanes were projected onto small screens surrounding the simulator's cockpit. These films gave pilots a better illusion of flight, but had the drawback of not being able to respond to the pilot's actions. After the war, however, the technology of televised images progressed far enough so that simulators could incorporate images from video cameras that "flew" over model airfields and countrysides as the student pilot controlled the simulator.

Electronic computers made their appearance in flight simulators after World War II. The military needed a way to record pilot performance for later review, in order to get as much effect from each training session as possible. Also, the military wanted a few trainers that could be programmed to simulate numerous airplanes, both to train pilots in as many planes as possible and to test designs as part of the development of new aircraft. As with the old Link Trainer, computerized simulators allowed novice pilots to gain basic experience without risking their lives or damaging airplanes worth thousands, and eventually millions, of dollars. As the technology became more sophisticated, the flying services started to use flight simulators to evaluate and hone experienced pilots' skills. But these simulators had their limits. They provided a narrow range of simulated airspace—the largest models were designed to represent only six square miles—and were not able to reproduce the extreme high-speed, high-energy maneuvers associated with midair dogfights or air-to-ground attack runs.

Moreover, the simulators were very expensive. Because each airplane in the nation's military had its own unique layout—from cockpit design to aerobatics—each had to have its own unique simulator to reproduce these variables, which added to the cost. Each simulator cost as much as a couple of its real-world counterparts (though cheaper than the cost of a few *real* wrecked airplanes). And when a particular type of airplane became obsolete and left service, the simulator had to be thrown away. This technological "fact of life" became even more of a problem in the 1960s, when pilots needed simulators that could help them keep pace with their increasingly sophisticated aircraft.

The military's drive to create better simulators was soon to overlap the efforts of another group—the computer scientists who were trying to make computers easier for people to use.

5

A NEW VIEW OF DATA

Sight defines how most people move through the world, and it is the main sense people use when they interact with computers. Beeps, bells, or other sounds can indicate a program is running or alert users to a problem, and some accessories provide a limited sense of touch for a small range of computer applications. However, computers present nearly all other information visually, from words within a text file to attacking monsters in a video game.

One of the most astonishing things about seeing Sketchpad and the On-Line System at work was the fact that people *could* see these innovative displays react instantly to commands. Thinking suddenly became something that they could do with the assistance of a computer monitor, not just within their heads. Naturally, many researchers who were attracted to this area of computing, as well as others who developed their own methods, sought new ways to show what data could look like.

"The Ultimate Display"

A few years before Douglas Engelbart's research group introduced text windows and mouse pointers to the world, Ivan Sutherland began working on a new computer-graphics display. Sketchpad had been a successful demonstration of what computer graphics could do, and, as head of IPTO, Sutherland knew about other projects that had similar goals. The work that these researchers were doing and the advances they made convinced him that people in the not-to-distant future would be able to interact more naturally with computers.

However, Sutherland was concerned about the tools and techniques people were creating to control information, including his own work. These new human-computer interfaces—the methods people relied on to work with computers—still required humans to adapt themselves to machinery. Sketchpad, for instance, had required people to sit in one spot, peck at a keyboard, and lean forward to draw figures on a small surface. Other systems put similar limits on how and where people could work.

Why not create computers that were designed to accommodate themselves to the way *humans* worked? Sutherland wondered. Given a choice, people would rather work directly with displayed information, rather than with tools that formed a barrier between them and the data. After thinking a while about what such a system could do, Sutherland set down his ideas in a short essay called "The Ultimate Display."

In the article, which he wrote in 1965, he proposed creating an immersive-visualization system that people could use the same way they used any object in the real world. Ideally, the display "would be a room within which the computer can control the existence of matter," he wrote. Objects in the room would be as "real" as anything outside the room, but the computer could change their shape or position on command. This type of display also could give people "a chance to gain familiarity with concepts not realizable in the physical world," such as mathematical or scientific theories.

Similar rooms had been proposed before, but as science fiction, not science fact. For example, "The Veldt," a 1950 short story by famed science-fiction author Ray Bradbury, was based in a room that displayed a realistic simulation of the African plains. And years after Sutherland published "The Ultimate Display," the idea of an immersive-environment room appeared again, as the "holodecks" of *Star Trek: The Next Generation* and similar television shows.

Following his own advice, Sutherland decided to build a *prototype*, or working model, of his "ultimate display." The idealized version—a computer that controlled matter within a room—was and still is impossible. However, Sutherland decided to create the next best thing: a head-mounted display that would immerse people in a world created using three-dimensional computer graphics. It was a big project. The Advanced Research Projects Agency provided money for the team of MIT researchers Sutherland put together in 1966. So did the Office of Naval Research, which saw the HMD's potential as a possible flight simulation tool.

Over the next five years, Sutherland and his team created the display system they nicknamed the Sword of Damocles. It got its name from the two-piece rod mounted on the ceiling that supported the display and which seemed to hang over people after they strapped their heads into the viewer. According to an ancient legend, a ruler of the Sicilian city of Syracuse once made a member of his court sit beneath a sword that hung by a single hair during a banquet. This command was meant to teach the courtier and others how risky it was to be a king. The head-mounted display was far less likely to injure its users, of course, but the sight of someone using it reminded people of the old story.

Forging the Sword of Damocles

Building the new display device was a tricky task. The team had to solve a series of technological challenges that no one ever had needed to deal with before. For one thing, they had to develop a reliable *tracking* method to tell the computer where a user was standing and looking. An attempt to use ultrasonic speakers and microphones did not work, as physical objects it the laboratory kept blocking the signal from reaching one or more microphones. Finally, the researchers devised the two-piece rod: It could expand and contract as its operator moved around, and it had movable linkages where it was attached to the ceiling and the HMD. Sensors in the rod and at both ends measured which way the user's head turned and how far he moved after strapping on the device. Though the rod was a cumbersome way to deal with the problem, the researchers figured that it would work well enough until they or some other group could come up with a better method.

Working out the details of the computer-graphics display also took a lot of work. The team had to design hardware and software to generate two slightly different images of the same object for each eye, while making sure that both images lined up correctly in the user's mind. They even had to work out some way to prevent the computer from displaying sections that would be hidden from the user's view in the real world, such as the far end of a solid cube. By 1970, Sutherland and his colleagues had conquered most of these obstacles. A group of computers generated objects, changed their appearance and position as users moved around, and created the illusion of solidity. The first

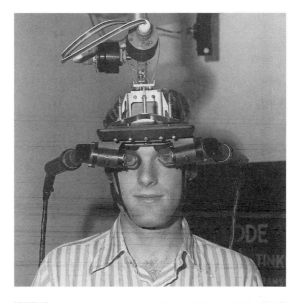

The Sword of Damocles (shown here at the University of Utah) was the first head-mounted display ever built to render computer-generated stereoscopic graphics. It also was one of the most cumbersome HMDs ever built: Its users had to strap themselves into it for the display's 3-D effect to work. [University of Utah/Evans & Sutherland Computer Corp.]

image that the system displayed was a wire-frame cube that seemed to hang in midair. Other images followed, including a molecule and a room that seemed to fit within the researchers' laboratory at the University of Utah (where Sutherland had moved a little while after starting work on the display).

The early 1970s marked the end of the Sword of Damocles project. Like Sketchpad and the On-Line System, the Sword of Damocles had shown what people could do with the right amount of computer assistance. It also exposed the students and faculty members who were part of Sutherland's team to the leading edge of their field of study. Many of these researchers used the knowledge they gained from their work to develop other aspects of computer technology, including the hardware and software in today's personal computers and the Internet. The display system itself, though, was too expensive and, with its support rod, too clumsy to be developed much further. Also, Sutherland and the head of the University of Utah's computer-graphics department, David Evans, had started their own computer-graphics company in Salt Lake City. After the Sword project met its goal, Sutherland left the university for the business world.

Computer Data that Can Be Touched

While the work of researchers like Sutherland and Engelbart had some of the greatest effect on the development of modern-day computers, virtual reality included, many other researchers worked on other aspects of human-computer interaction starting in the mid-1960s. Their goals were not always just to build better visual displays. Touch is a key sense in immersive environments, and a lot of researchers started out trying to create touch-oriented, or haptic, displays.

Beginning in the late 1960s, at the University of North Carolina's Chapel Hill campus, a team led by Dr. Frederick Brooks—a former IBM computer programmer who had become interested in the human factors side of computing—worked on a way to study chemicals using *force-feedback* simulations. Force-feedback devices use motors to resist or push back against movement from their operators. By varying the amount of resistance or opposing force the motors generate, these devices can create the impression that the user is moving or handling physical objects.

Part of Brooks's inspiration to delve into touch-oriented computing came from Ivan Sutherland's work. In particular, Brooks was captivated by a comment Sutherland made during a speech in 1965, the same year of "The Ultimate Display." Sutherland had mentioned that people should be able to use their hands not just to type letters or turn knobs, but also to control computers with natural gestures such as pointing and grasping. In fact, the computers that generated the Sword of Damocles' environment also supported the use of a control wand, nicknamed the "Sorcerer's Apprentice," that people could use to create and manipulate images in midair. Shaped like grip of a pistol or a joystick, the wand had four control buttons and a couple of other controls, as well as a small position sensor. Using the wand and a "wall chart" of commands that appeared in the HMD, it was possible to draw objects, stick them together, stretch or shrink them, and perform other seemingly magical feats.

Brooks thought that the idea of grabbing onto computer data was too good to pass up. However, he realized that creating this type of interface would succeed only if the work focused on a real-life task. Brooks decided to pursue his research on touch-oriented computing by creating models of proteins and other biochemical molecules. He and other researchers at the Chapel Hill campus began exploring ways to simulate the forces that hold molecules together or cause them to fly apart and to give computer users the impression that they were physically touching an object that existed only as computer data.

The easiest way to create the illusion of touch, the Carolina researchers discovered, was through *force-feedback* simulations. This method provided a comparatively simple and compact mechanism for interacting with simulated objects. Better still, it was a method that the researchers could pursue using technology that was available at the time. Creating force-feedback manipulators was simply a matter of assembling the motors, pulleys, and other components, and attaching them to a computer that could translate the digital data into varying levels of force. One of the most ambitious projects that Brooks and his team took on, called GROPE-II, used a ceiling mounted, motorized handgrip to handle computer-graphics building blocks. Unfortunately, Brooks developed GROPE-II in the early 1970s, a time when computers still did not have very much computing power. The ability to stack on-screen building blocks was a respectable achievement for its time, but it was a far cry from being able to reproduce the complex effects of molecular chemistry. Even so, Brooks still thought that GROPE would be a valuable computer interface tool once computers in general had advanced far enough. So he decided to work on other areas of human-computer interaction, putting off further work on GROPE-II until computer technology caught up.

Putting People in Artificial Realities

Computer researchers and inventors had tried other methods of physically manipulating data in the 1970s. Toward the beginning of the decade, a computer scientist and artist named Myron Krueger wondered if there might not be a better way to use computers than to strap on bulky, inconvenient appliances. Why go to that much trouble? Why not, he speculated, make computers that watched and responded to humans without any tools?

Krueger already had experimented with this type of human-computer interaction. In 1969, he had helped build a physical, computer-controlled artistic environment at the University of Wisconsin at Madison that responded to people who entered the area. Called GLOWFLOW, the display was a darkened room with pressure-sensitive floor pads, water-filled glass tubes, and a synthesizer whose speakers were placed along the walls. Walking about the space caused lights in the tubes to switch on and off, while the synthesizer played different sound effects. A year later, he designed METAPLAY, which used a large video screen and a hidden video camera to surround images of its visitors with different types of graphics displays. METAPLAY's control room was in an office a quarter of a mile away from the on-campus art gallery. While the exhibit was running, someone (often Krueger) used a specialized computer and an early *graphics tablet* to draw designs around the audience members.

In 1974, after constructing other interactive video exhibits, Krueger decided to concentrate on creating computers that responded solely to the movements of a user's image in an on-screen computer-graphics environment. He put together a system that projected the user's silhouette onto a large video screen. Using the video image, the computer monitored what the user did and changed the display around the image according to how he or she moved. One option this system provided was a sort of finger-painting routine. By extending his or her index finger, the user could draw colored lines all over the video screen. Erasing the design was a matter of simply spreading his or her hand wide open.

This system, which Krueger named VIDEOPLACE, was one of the first examples of what Krueger himself called *artificial reality (AR)*. He envisioned AR as a computer environment that responded to its user directly, rather than through any special bit of clothing. By simply placing the user's image in a computer display, the computer would provide the user with all that he or she needed to control the computer. AR would be a more natural, intuitive interface.

Another attempt at this type of projected computer reality was the "Put That There" system developed in the mid-1970s at the MIT Media Lab, which researchers at the university established to create prototypes—preferably, ones that could become sellable products—of futuristic technology. This system's unusual name came from the spoken-word command its developers used most often. A user would sit in front of the system's display screen, which might, for example, display the image of a ship floating on an ocean. Pointing to the ship, the user would say, "Put that." Pointing to another area of the ocean, the user would say, "There," at which the computer would move the image of the ship to its new location.

Two devices made this interaction possible. The first device was a voice monitor the Media Lab researchers created that allowed the computer to recognize spoken commands. The computer could understand a limited number of words—*put*, *that*, and *there* were about as much as the device could handle—but it was enough for the system to work. Indeed, this device was one of the first successful voice-recognition peripherals ever used in a computer.

A company called Polhemus Navigation Systems made the second device, a magnetic position sensor about the size of a couple of sugar cubes that could be attached to the back of the user's hand. In the Media Room laboratory that housed "Put That There," a researcher would sit in a chair near a small magnetic field generator, facing the screen. No matter where the user's hand was, one sensor would be closer to the source of the field and would receive a stronger signal than the other. As the sensors moved around, the "Put That There" computer combined their signals and calculated where the user's hand was. At that point, it was a simple matter for the computer to figure out where in the display the user was pointing or even if the user's hand was outside the display area.

Because of all this experimental and artistic work, most of the technology that would lead to the development of virtual reality was in place. The crossover between the efforts of engineers who wanted to create better computer controls and engineers who wanted to build better flight simulators was about to happen.

6

A NEW COURSE FOR INDOOR FLIGHT TRAINING

Airplanes, and the flight simulators that imitated them, developed more rapidly than computers did. After the end of World War II, jet engines replaced propellers in fighters, bombers, and low-altitude attack aircraft; commercial jet travel began toward the end of the 1950s. As fighter craft became faster, dogfights began to take up larger patches of the sky; rockets and missiles took over from machine guns as the main air-to-air weapon at the pilot's command. When radar systems and advanced electronics were perfected for use in military and commercial airplanes, they gave pilots information about their aircraft and the skies around them that pilots in previous decades only dreamed of having.

All these innovations came at a cost, however, and not just in terms of a nation's military budget. With their radar displays, flight data gauges, weapons controls, and other devices, modern aircraft were requiring pilots to choose from too many options. Fighter pilots in particular were having to find and operate too many controls to keep their planes in the air, stay out of harm's way, and still be able to strike at enemy air and/or ground targets.

Military aircraft designers tried to make the job of flying easier for the pilots. Heads-up displays (HUDs) helped a lot. These were small clear panels on top of a fighter's or an attack plane's control console that displayed crucial information such as altitude, speed, and enemy plane positions at eye level, without blocking the pilot's view forward. The panels reflected the information much as a double-paned window can reflect the image of a person looking through it. During a dogfight, HUDs gave pilots the ability to focus and fire on their opponents without looking away to check instruments.

Designers also moved many of an airplane's controls and switches onto the handles of the cockpit's joystick and throttle controls, where they would be easier to reach. This "hands-on-throttle-and-stick," or HOTAS, method drastically reduced the amount of time pilots had to take their hands off these controls to select weapons, scan for enemy aircraft, or perform other tasks. This was an important advance in safety as well as convenience: Every time a pilot lets loose of a control, he or she runs the risk of losing control of the aircraft even when the skies seem clear.

Naturally, flight simulators copied these innovations, and when computers that could handle the task of simulating flight came along, they were incorporated into the training machines. By the early 1970s, computers had reached the point where they could generate computer graphics for flight simulators, replacing the limited range of miniaturized video cameras. In fact, one of the first companies to create computer-graphics displays for military simulators was Evans & Sutherland, the business that Ivan Sutherland and David Evans started while Sutherland was finishing work on the Sword of Damocles.

Various flying services around the world started developing systems that combined cockpit mock-ups with computer graphics. One such system, built for the U.S. Navy by General Electric Company, surrounded a fighter cockpit with three large screens. Special projectors placed behind these screens projected images of the sky, the sea, and enemy airplanes. Commercial airline pilots, who had been training in mock-ups of the passenger jetliners they flew, began to see computer-graphics scenes out the windows of their flight simulators as well.

An Overwhelming Interface

For military pilots, however, the HUDs and HOTAS controls in their cockpits did not eliminate the basic problem of flying modern jet aircraft. With their almost overwhelming numbers of controls and displays, modern airplanes had an interface that was not truly suited for their human operators. The military still needed a better way for pilots to control their planes. And new pilots needed a comparable method for safely learning how to operate their planes before taking to the skies.

One of the people who looked for a solution to these problems was Dr. Thomas Furness III, a researcher at the United States Air Force's Wright-Patterson Air Force Base in Ohio. "It was clear that we weren't going to get there by using highly coded instruments in the cockpit, and that these crew members were having to spend too much time translating what was on the instruments to what was going on in the world," Furness recalled.

Furness thought of a better way to present information to pilots in the early 1970s. As he and other researchers saw the problem, pilots had to deal with too many dials, displays, and switches, all of which had to be small enough and close enough together to fit in the tight space of the cockpit. The solution? Eliminate the physical displays. Rather than force the pilots to divide their attention between scanning the skies and focusing on instruments in their cockpits, give them a simplified, all-inclusive computer display that would provide them with all the information they needed.

Furness had been involved in this type of research since 1966, when, as an air force enlisted man, he joined a team of Wright-Patterson researchers that was formed to take the heads-up display off the cockpit console and place it on the pilot's helmet. The researchers believed that suspending the display right in front of the eyes would make it easier for pilots to maintain situational awareness, the ability to judge how things were going in the world around them and how to respond to threats. To achieve their goal, the team had to figure out how to shrink the HMD and automatically adjust the display to match up with the real world as a pilot looked around.

This was a tremendous project to take on in the 1960s. This was a time when people still used punched cards to enter data in many computer systems, and when computers that responded instantly, in "real time," were expensive pieces of specialized equipment. For their project to succeed, the team Furness had joined had to build computers that were fast enough to display stable images in the virtual space of the helmet-mounted displays. They also had to figure out a method to detect exactly which way the pilot was looking and to come up with a display that the pilot could read whether he was looking at a bright blue sky or a dark cloud bank.

The team met these challenges by forcing technology to do things it had not been designed to do, aided by a large research budget from the air force. They built computers that could handle the display task and were small enough to fit inside an airplane. The researchers designed HMD that was similar to the Sword of Damocles, with special cathode-ray tubes to create images for the pilot and lenses that could direct the image into the pilot's eyes. The group also experimented with different types of position trackers, including one that used a series of infrared lights and detectors.

"We were pushing the envelope to get the first technology out there that would do this," Furness said.

As they devised a way to place computer-generated images within a pilot's real-world view, the researchers were learning never-before-known details about how the eyes work. To make sure the images stood out well enough against the real world, the team had to learn what happens to images that are beamed directly onto the retina, how the images stimulate the rod and cone receptors, how the eye adjusts to sudden flashes of bright light, and other facts about how the eyes work. This knowledge helped advance the development of the display.

By the late 1960s, after years of development and testing on the ground, the Wright-Patterson research group had a system that was ready to take to the skies in a series of experimental flight tests. When the pilots who took part in these tests came back to Earth, they reported that the new display more than lived up to its designers' promises.

"As a matter of fact, it dramatically expanded the capability of existing weapons systems we had on board these aircraft, just by providing better ways of interfacing with those weapons systems," Furness said.

"Darth Vader" in the Cockpit

The helmet display system had performed successfully, proving that computer-generated displays would work in flight and showing that the researchers were on the right path. In 1973, Furness suggested taking the concept to the next level. Instead of simply projecting a digital image that merged with the physical world, the air force needed to create a three-dimensional environment that showed pilots where they were and what was happening, while filtering out all but the most important details.

This level of human augmentation went far beyond the ideas behind the Sword of Damocles or the mouse-and-window On-Line System. Though all three displays had a similar purpose—to let humans use machines as thinking tools—Furness said these projects had little else in common:

> Ivan Sutherland, Douglas Engelbart, and myself were pursuing these things independently for different reasons. As it turns out, we were laying the foundational pieces for the technology (of immersive computing)—in terms of military technology, one that would allow us to build these helmet-mounted sights and helmet-mounted displays. And in the process of building these, we (Wright-Patterson researchers) began to realize that you could . . . create, basically, a virtual cockpit, where the whole cockpit was projected, and not just a small piece of it.

Wright-Patterson was not the only research center in the drive to build these next-generation aircraft displays, either. For example, the McDonnell-Douglas Aircraft Corporation, one of the United States's oldest airplane manufacturers, developed a head-mounted display for the United States Navy in the mid-to-late 1970s as part of its Virtual Takeoff and Landing, or VITAL, simulator. As its name suggests, VITAL was designed to help F-18 pilots in the U.S. Navy learn how to take off from and land on runways and aircraft carriers. The VITAL helmet was a regulation military pilot's helmet with a metal framework that supported the simulator's optics. Like the Sword of Damocles and the Wright-Patterson HUD helmet, VITAL had two cathode-ray tubes that projected computer displays into the pilot's eye using a set of prisms. The helmet worked, but it was cumbersome and hard to use, which defeated the purpose.

Furness started working on the proposal for his all-inclusive computer display, the Visually Coupled Airborne Systems Simulator (VCASS, for short) in 1973, and received both approval to start the project and money to pay for it in 1977. Over the next five years, he and a group of colleagues refined his ideas, once again building many of the components they needed and using existing technology in unique ways. Even the computers that generated and controlled the graphics in the HMD were hand-modified, special-use machines that were at least as powerful as some commercially available supercomputers around the same time.

Correctly monitoring the pilot's head as he looked around was even more important for the new display than it had been in the 1960s. After all, pilots could switch off or disregard the display in the older HMD in case of malfunction or emergency. VCASS, though, was supposed to take the place of a traditional helmet, and it had to show pilots exactly what was in front of their eyes. Furness and his team tried many types of head tracking: infrared lights and detectors, similar to the ones used in modern television remote controls; optical sensors; ultrasonic speakers and microphones; and electromagnetic trackers similar to those used by the MIT "Put That There" display. In the end, the electromagnetic trackers—which, like MIT's, were made by Polhemus—proved to be the most reliable.

In 1981, Furness switched on his VCASS for the first time. It featured a huge bug-eyed helmet that contained a pair of high-resolution computer display screens, a stereophonic sound system, and a microphone that allowed pilots to give spoken commands to the computer that was running the simulation. The simulator's helmet detected which way the pilot moved his head by monitoring a magnetic field generated by a nearby transmitter. Based on these measurements, the computer changed the scene being displayed to match what the pilot would see in real life.

The images displayed by the helmet were simple, yet they gave the pilots who wore it enough information to control the simulated airplane and to complete the simulated mission. The landscape the pilot "flew" over was a simple two-color checkerboard. Colored triangles, boxes, and cylinders represented friendly and hostile airplanes, buildings, and enemy radar envelopes. In the foreground, an airplane-shaped space contained a handful of gauges that monitored fuel level, speed, and other necessary information. Pictures of missiles and bombs indicated which weapons systems were armed and which were on standby.

The VCASS caught the attention of the air force officers who were assigned to evaluate it, not in the least part because of its unusual look. The helmet, with its huge oval display screens and insectoid appearance, looked like the villain Darth Vader in the *Star Wars* movies. But the Darth Vader helmet also earned the respect of the air force pilots who were asked to test it, because of the true-to-life nature of its seemingly simplistic display. Furness said:

> These were all still one-of-a-kind systems. But in 1981, we proved that you could indeed build a virtual cockpit and make it highly interactive using a combination of hand position, eye position, speech, three-dimensional representation of information, and so forth.
>
> That became our workhorse to continue on where we launched, in the mid-1980s, the so-called SuperCockpit program, which was a very well-funded project to continue to develop the bits and pieces that would allow us to create these immersive environments.

SuperCockpit was an advanced version of VCASS that the air force asked Furness to develop. It had half-silvered mirrors that gave pilots a view of the real world and the virtual environment simultaneously. A three-dimensional sound-effects system helped pilots locate virtual targets in the "air." An eye tracker inside the helmet monitored where a pilot was looking within the virtual environment, allowing him to pick out targets without having to push a button. A basic voice-recognition system gave pilots the ability to fire weapons with a code word. And there even was a means of creating virtual tactile controls, using gloves imbedded with tiny crystals that vibrated when an electric current switched on.

With the creation of the SuperCockpit, all of the elements of virtual reality had been assembled. There was a head-mounted display that could show three-dimensional environments and a computer system that could generate those environments. The computer could tell

The Visually Coupled Airborne Systems Simulator, or VCASS, combined a fighter cockpit simulator with a fully immersive digital environment projected in the head-mounted display this pilot is wearing. Because of its appearance, the HMD was nicknamed the "Darth Vader" helmet.
(United States Air Force)

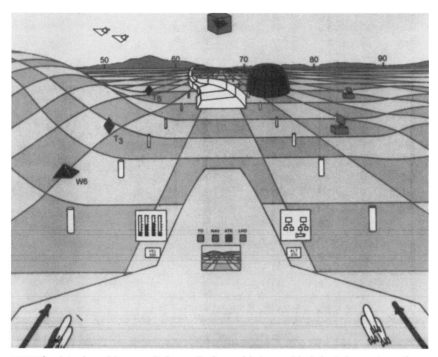

VCASS's virtual world was a fighter pilot's world; it provided the information pilots needed to maneuver, avoid simulated ground threats, and prevail against enemy aircraft. [United States Air Force]

where someone was within that environment and change the display according to where he traveled. While the pilots who experimented with the SuperCockpit could not grab hold or alter any of the objects within the environment (aside from blowing them out of the sky), they did have the sensation of feeling triggers or buttons they pressed that were displayed in midair. Finally, it seemed that computers were going to become true assistants to human beings, rather than just computational tools.

7

MIMICKING REALITY

After two decades of research into and development of better tools for using computers, virtual reality arrived in 1986 with Super-Cockpit at Wright-Patterson Air Force Base. However, SuperCockpit was just about the only virtual-environment technology that existed. There were a handful of other programs elsewhere in the world, but none of them provided as advanced a level of immersion in their computer-generated environments. And, in fact, the term *virtual reality* had not yet been developed to describe the new technology. It would be another few years before the phrase became part of the language.

SuperCockpit, the most sophisticated immersive computing system in the world, also was the most expensive. Pushing the boundaries of technology always has been costly, and developing the VCASS helmet and the other tools had pushed the boundaries far beyond the point anyone imagined they could go. Also, it was a military-sponsored project. Its funding came from the Department of Defense, which had a large budget for developing new tools to fight the cold war against the Soviet Union. So, how much of an effort did it take to pull VCASS together? Consider this: According to one story, when another computer-graphics researcher asked to buy just the VCASS helmet, he learned that it would cost $1 million.

As expensive at it was, SuperCockpit's debut as a working prototype came at a good time. In the mid-1980s, computers were appearing in all areas of life, not just in universities, government offices, and big corporations. People and small businesses had been buying *microcomputers* built by companies such as Apple Computer Inc. and Radio Shack to use as word processors, accounting tools, and teaching aids. When IBM brought out a minicomputer in 1981 that it called the PC, short for *personal computer*, people began using the term for all of these small-size information processors. At the end of 1982, *Time* magazine named the computer as its "Machine of the Year," and in 1984, Apple introduced its first Macintosh computer, which had a single-button mouse and a *graphical user interface*, or GUI, which used icons instead of *command lines* to list and launch programs.

People were becoming accustomed to computers in other ways as well. Video games had appeared a decade earlier with the release of PONG, a very simple table tennis game, in 1974. As computer graphics improved, video games became more sophisticated, and people came to expect more amazing effects each time they went into a video arcade. Home video consoles also introduced people to the idea of having a computer in their living room or bedroom. A couple of companies even allowed people to connect their consoles over the telephone and play against people living in different cities, as a sort of preliminary step toward modern-day on-line games.

Small groups of computer professionals and hobbyists were developing new, creative ways to use these technological appliances. In the mid-1980s, for instance, two video-game programmers were trying to build a system that allowed people to program computers without using a keyboard. Jaron Lanier and Thomas Zimmerman were colleagues at the Atari Research Center in Sunnyvale, California, a town near Stanford University. Atari Inc. was one of the world's major video-game manufacturers, and it had opened the research facility to create the new, advanced games that would keep them on top of the market. Many other companies had set high-technology research centers and factories in the area stretching from Palo Alto to San Jose—so many, in fact, that the area became known as Silicon Valley.

Zimmerman had developed and patented a control glove that would turn a computer into a music synthesizer—essentially, it was an air guitar that actually played music. Each finger of the glove was rigged with a small flexible tube that carried light from tiny lamps to light-sensing *photoreceptors*. As the wearer bent his or her fingers, the amount of light that reached the photoreceptor changed and varied the signal that the sensor sent to the computer. The computer thus measured how far each finger bent and responded with the sound a guitar would make as its strings were strummed.

Lanier, who shared Zimmerman's interest in music, also saw Zimmerman's glove as a potential computer-programming tool for people who were not professional programmers. Lanier had a pet project of his own called Mandala, a system that used symbols to represent computer-programming codes. These symbols—which included kangaroos and ice cubes—formed another type of graphical user interface, one that showed people how the computer codes that the symbols represented were making the computer operate. Lanier believed that linking these symbols together would give people a faster, more natural way of interacting with their computers and turn more people into programmers.

Zimmerman's glove offered a perfect way to manipulate these icons. With a properly rigged wired glove, Lanier thought, people could physically grab symbols as they needed them and link them together like beads on a string. Lanier suggested that Zimmerman attach a position tracker to the back of the glove to let computers track where it moved as well as how far its fingers bent. The two men decided to develop the glove on their own and left Atari in 1983. Using money Lanier had earned for designing an extremely popular game called Moondust, the programmers started their own firm, which they called VPL Research. (Supposedly, "VPL" comes from "visual programming language," another term that described Mandala.) They improved the flex sensors on Zimmerman's glove by using *optical fibers* rather than flexible tubes to conduct light. They also added the magnetic tracker that Lanier had suggested. When they finished, they named the device the DataGlove and began selling it, though not as a tool for a visual programming language.

Remaking Reality at NASA

Myron Krueger's artificial reality, Thomas Furness's VCASS and SuperCockpit work, the DataGlove with its magnetic tracker, and the desire to manipulate computer data by hand were all fated to come together in another area of Silicon Valley around 1985. The man who brought them together was a scientist with the National Aeronautics and Space Administration (NASA), Michael McGreevy, who had been searching for a way to examine three-dimensional objects using computer graphics.

NASA scientists have always been able to come up with unique ways to display data. In the 1960s, NASA sent Surveyor, an unmanned probe, to the Moon to send back images in preparation for the upcoming Apollo missions. To get a "lander's-eye view" of the Moon, NASA scientists glued the images the Surveyor sent back to the inside of a hollow sphere that had a hole at the bottom. By standing with their heads inside the sphere, the scientists could see a view of the Moon as it looked from the Surveyor's landing site. The globe provided a two-dimensional view of the Moon's three-dimensional environment, but it allowed the scientists to get an impression of the terrain that they could not get simply by looking at flat photographs.

Up through the early 1980s, though, there seemed to be no way to replicate three-dimensional environments, aside from building dioramas. Then McGreevy heard about VCASS and the work Thomas Furness had done with three-dimensional computer graphics. McGreevy was intrigued; he thought he could adapt such a system to a host of engineering, design, and exploration projects where he worked, at the NASA-Ames Research Center on the southern tip of the San Francisco Bay. The only problem was the expense involved in buying or building the type of HMD that Furness had created in Ohio. NASA did not have that kind of money to spend on experimental computer displays.

So McGreevy and his colleagues did what engineers have always done when confronted with an impossible situation: They worked around it. In 1984, McGreevy's team decided to create a display that might not be as clear as VCASS but would be far less expensive. In addition to the rise of personal computers, the 1980s also were a boom time for personal electronics, such as portable radios and tape players. By 1984, an electronics company was selling another type of extremely interesting personal technology—a pint-sized television set that featured a two-inch-square *liquid-crystal display* (LCD) instead of a cathode-ray tube (CRT).

Here was a solution to at least part of the problem McGreevy faced. One of the reasons that the Darth Vader helmet was so expensive was that it used cutting-edge CRT technology to create extremely clear color images. The black-and-white LCD screens did not give as sharp a picture—their images were made up of tiny dots—but the whole TV set, including the displays and their controlling circuits, cost only a few hundred dollars.

The Ames researchers bought a pair of the handheld TV sets, removed the screens, and wired them into a frame that looked like a scuba mask. They connected this setup to a group of linked computers, including two from Evans & Sutherland, that sent images to the LCD screens. A set of special wide-angle lenses called LEEP (Large Expanse, Extra Perspective) optics, made by a Massachusetts company called LEEP Systems Inc., made the images easier to see. The team also attached a Polhemus magnetic-position sensor to the mask to allow the computer to track which way the mask pointed. When they finished assembling these pieces, McGreevy and his colleagues had a three-dimensional computer-graphics viewer that cost only $2,000.

McGreevy dubbed this new display VIVED, short for Virtual Visual Environment Display. Like Sutherland's Sword of Damocles and Furness's VCASS helmet, VIVED tricked the user's brain into perceiving a computer display as a three-dimensional world. One of the first environments it displayed was an air-traffic control simulation in which wire-frame airplanes floated above a square grid that was meant to represent the ground. While wearing the VIVED HMD, observers could walk around each airplane, inspecting it from all sides. Because VIVED was so inexpensive compared to other displays, it received a great deal of interest from university researchers, computer manufacturers, and others who realized the benefits of having a three-dimensional computer display.

But VIVED, as far as McGreevy's group was concerned, was still a work in progress. As impressive as it was, it had a number of drawbacks. The displayed objects did not move; there was no way to interact with them, to shift them around, or to change their design. Looking at the airplanes was like looking at a sculpture locked inside a glass cabinet. The design team needed to find a way to improve the display.

A New View of Computer Data

One of the first people to buy a DataGlove from VPL Research was Scott Fisher, another former Atari programmer who had gone to work at the Ames Research Center with McGreevy's VIVED group. Fisher figured out that adding the DataGlove would give VIVED the interactive dimension that its creators desired. He sought to expand VIVED even further by adding a spoken-word command system and three-dimensional sound. Voice-recognition software was already available, having been used in such projects as the MIT Media Lab's

"Put That There." Three-dimensional sound was a little more difficult. Simply adding a stereophonic sound system to the HMD would
not work. While stereo speakers can move music and sound effects
from left to right, they do so in what amounts to a flat plane. They do
not give the effect of sounds originating from an object or staying with
that object as it moves around.

Fortunately for Fisher, it was possible by 1985 to create three-
dimensional-sound simulators that could enhance the VIVED display.
Crystal River Engineering, a California company that produced computer sound devices, developed a system that wrapped sounds around
the user and added the illusion of depth. The VIVED team incorporated the device, which Crystal River named the Convolvotron, into its
system in 1987.

With the addition of sound effects, spoken-word commands, and
the ability to manipulate virtual worlds, VIVED was no longer just a
visual display. It was a self-contained workstation; people could use it
far more easily than they could type arcane codes on keyboards while
looking at two-dimensional TV screens. What is more important, the
new system caused a shift in the way people thought about how
humans could interact with computers. The system needed a new
name to reflect this technological advance and its accompanying shift
in thinking. Thus, its developers called their creation the Virtual Interactive Environment Workstation—VIEW.

The VIEW was as much a revolution in adaptability as it was a revolution in technology. People who saw it realized they could do any
task that could be represented as a virtual environment. It was not a
perfect system, though. Even in its final form, there was much to be
desired with VIEW. For one thing, its graphics displays were very
primitive. At first, VIEW could only display wire-frame objects, and at
a level of resolution so poor that one researcher said a person whose
vision was that bad in real life would be declared legally blind. VIEW
also took a long time playing "catch up" with its users: quickly turning
one's head started a series of stuttering environment shifts in the visual
display. More than anything, this lag time hurt the sense of immersion
VIEW created.

These drawbacks were more than balanced by VIEW's two main
advantages: It was cheap, and it worked. The entire VIEW hardware
suite cost less than $10,000, a significant saving over VCASS's mil-
lion-dollar helmet. The system could be applied to a host of projects,
from the original VIVED air-traffic simulation to a simulation of an
astronaut maneuvering back to a space shuttle. And despite the grainy,

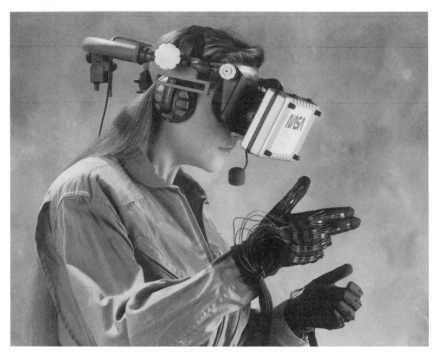

The Virtual Interactive Environment Workstation (VIEW) was the first fully functional virtual-reality display in history. It paired VIVED's stereoscopic head-mounted display with three-dimensional sound, a pair of wired gloves, and a speech-recognition system, thrusting the user into a self-contained virtual world.
[Courtesy National Aeronautics and Space Administration [Ames Research Center]]

fuzzy images that the LCD screens provided, VIEW *did* create a believable, if not flawless, sense of immersion.

Naming the New Wave of Computing

The development of VIEW marked the creation of virtual reality in many people's minds, though nobody really knew how popular it might become. There were questions about whether or not this new technology could be reproduced cheaply enough for other people to buy and use it. There even was a brief time when nobody knew exactly what to *call* it. Should it be called "artificial reality," the term Myron Krueger had used for more than a decade to refer to his immersive environments? Would calling it "virtual-environment technology" (VET) be more accurate? In the end, a 1988 article on Jaron Lanier and VPL popularized the term virtual reality. Lanier used the term while he was describing a product based on an improved version of VIEW that was called RB2, short for Reality Built For Two.

RB2, the world's first commercially produced VR system, ran off an Apple Macintosh computer. The Macintosh controlled two other computers designed by Silicon Graphics Inc., a company that made highly advanced graphics-oriented computers. It came with one or two sets of DataGloves and one or two EyePhones, VPL's version of the 3-D head-mounted display created for VIEW. Later, VPL developed a full-body version of the DataGlove called, appropriately, the DataSuit.

As with all new technologies, RB2 had many drawbacks. One of these drawbacks was its price: It cost more than $400,000 for two people to share the virtual-reality experience. (A one-person version cost a mere $225,000.) It also shared many of the image-quality and body-tracking problems of the VIEW system. However, it showed people around the world that the technology worked and could adapt its abilities to their needs. Soon, researchers and entrepreneurs in the United States and abroad began developing their own methods of mimicking reality. Universities began to include VR classes among their advanced computing courses and established research and development programs for immersive-environment technology. It seemed that virtual reality would become the future of computing, and people wanted to take part. Over the next few years, a host of laboratories and companies refined these tools and developed new ones that provided the sensation of immersive computing.

8

REALITY SIMULATORS: SUPERCOMPUTERS TO PCs

People may experience the world through their five senses, but these senses do not create a three-dimensional worldview by themselves. It is the brain's job to blend the information of the senses into an overall picture of the physical world. Just as the brain is the center of the biological system that allows people to perceive reality, computers are the center of the electronic system that tricks the brain into perceiving artificial environments as real. These computers, sometimes called *reality simulators* or *reality engines*, make up one side of the virtual-reality equation that yields successful immersion. The other side includes the *effectors*, the input and output devices that people use to work with computer-generated objects.

Reality simulators generate and draw, or *render,* the highly detailed images of virtual environments and rapidly change how the environments look or behave in response to the user's actions. As people work, the computers add any sounds and calculate any touch-related, or *tactile,* effects that are programmed into the simulation. In the end, the success or failure of a person's experience in one of these digital environments depends on the ability of the reality simulator to carry out the instructions of the virtual world's programmers.

Putting Reality in a Box

The first reality simulators were either custom-made or commercially produced computers that researchers modified themselves. In either case, they cost a lot of money, tens or even hundreds of thousands of dollars, depending on the type of work they had to do. Flight simulators in particular used some of the most advanced computers of their time, as they still do, to create the illusion of flying a real airplane. Some experimental systems, such as the ones developed for VCASS, used strictly one-of-a-kind computers. Other researchers held down the cost of their work by using older computers that were just good enough to demonstrate the idea of what a more sophisticated system could do. Each of the three computers that ran the VIVED head-mounted display, for example, was 15 years old.

Finding or building computers that could create a virtual environment was just the first step. Researchers also had to figure out a way to coordinate these machines and their various accessories. For a virtual-reality system to work correctly, all of its parts have to perform correctly at the same time. Adding effectors required somebody to work out a way to wire the devices into the computer's circuitry, as well as somebody to sit down and write a program telling the computer what to do with the new signals it was receiving.

This situation started changing in the early 1990s, when a number of companies began selling virtual-reality gear. By then, computer graphics had been a strong field of computing, apart from any immersive computing applications, for more than two decades. Computer-graphics effects had showed up in movies, car and airplane manufacturers were using computer-aided design programs to plan new vehicles, and some researchers were using computers to create scientific images, such as the structure of molecules. Much of this work was being done on special-purpose *workstations*, very powerful microcomputers that had large monitors and other accessories to make the work easier. These workstations already could create three-dimensional images by the time head-mounted displays and other effectors were invented, and the companies that made the workstations began adapting them to the new virtual-environment technology.

Over the next decade, many existing computer-graphics companies, such as Evans & Sutherland and Silicon Graphics Inc., adapted their existing computers for virtual-reality applications and designed new ones that could handle VR and other advanced graphics jobs. Other companies went into business specifically to produce VR machines. Today, some of these companies—the ones for which VR supplemented their already strong computer-graphics sales—still are in business. Some others went out of business when the market for virtual-reality products did not grow as fast as many people had expected.

At the same time, computer technology progressed to the point where even low-cost computers could generate some of the sensations of more expensive immersive computing systems. By 1995, books on designing digital worlds were providing guidelines on how to get into virtual reality as a hobby for $15,000—still a lot of money, but nowhere near the $300,000 it cost for a system in the late 1980s. These days, almost any computer can provide some, if not all, of the sensations of VR.

Levels of Reality Engines

A rule of thumb in computer science says that computers double in power about every two years. That is, each new series of computers works twice as fast, can handle twice as many functions at one time, and in general is twice as good as the series that represented "the state of the art" two years before. (Gordon Moore, one of the cofounders of computer chip maker Intel Corporation, first made this observation during the 1960s; ever since, it has been called Moore's Law.) This rapid progression is part of the reason why, for example, a handheld computer like a personal digital assistant can do more in the year 2002 than desktop computers costing a couple of thousand dollars could do in 1992.

Personal computers first were called microcomputers because they were far smaller than room-sized mainframes or table-sized *minicomputers*, smaller machines that appeared in the 1960s when transistors came into use. PCs also are called *general-purpose* computers, as are many larger computers, because they can perform a wide range of tasks without needing a large amount of special modifications. The same computer one person uses to write a book can, with a change of software, turn into a small-business accounting and inventory system or become a tool to create advertising graphics. PCs can become more powerful and versatile if they are part of a network that links a series of computers together or connects a group of PCs to a more powerful *server*. With such a network, computer users can transfer files from one machine to another and use more than one

CPU to carry out a task. In these types of networks, each PC is called a *terminal* or a *workstation*.

People have used personal computers as reality engines since the early days of VR, when linking two or three PCs together would supply enough calculating power to generate digitized worlds and provide stereoscopic vision. Over the years, a number of companies have built effectors such as head-mounted displays and wired gloves for personal computers. Other companies have designed VR-style accessories that display and control video games, which people have adapted for use in more sophisticated environments. However, while personal computers are capable of displaying very advanced computer graphics, they still are a bit underpowered for anything more than simple 3-D interaction.

The word *workstation* also refers to a type of microcomputer that is designed for tasks too complicated for a general-purpose computer, even one that is part of a network, to handle. In a sense, these workstations are souped-up personal computers that have some of the most powerful microprocessors available and a series of preprocessors and other components that speed up their work. The main operating software of a workstation also is more advanced than that of a personal computer; it has to be, in order to make full use of the workstation's components. The software can be based on a version of UNIX—a computer language that allows programmers to create complex applications using simple commands—or a few other programming languages designed for specific fields, such as science or engineering.

Like personal computers, workstations are built for one person to use at a time, and many workstations can be linked to one another and to a central mainframe computer. People use these computers, linked or by themselves, for medical, engineering, architectural, and other tasks that require high levels of computer graphics. Because they are ideally suited for complex calculation and rendering tasks, workstations often are the engines that drive sophisticated virtual environments.

At some point, however, the requirements of a virtual environment or three-dimensional simulation go beyond the limits of what even a network-linked workstation can do. Such high-level computing includes scientific research into global climate modeling and surgical simulation, weapons testing and design, and improvements in virtual-environment technology itself. Here is where supercomputers come in. Supercomputers are the most powerful and fastest mainframe computers that are available at any one time. They contain many multiple processors and huge amounts of memory. They also carry the largest price tags, putting them out of the reach of all but a few government agencies, research universities, and major corporations. Depending on the tasks they are designed to do, supercomputers can require their own specially designed software.

Whichever type of computer is chosen to house the virtual world, all follow similar patterns when creating the environment and presenting it to its users.

Inside a Reality Simulator

A powerful computer can make a poor reality simulator if it cannot display changes to the virtual environment quickly. For a simulation to work, there needs to be no delay, or *lag time*, between a user's action and its effect on the environment. In other words, the computer must perform and run faster than a human can look around or move within the virtual world. This is asking a lot of the computer. In order for it to adjust to human actions, the computer constantly has to check the status of position sensors, buttons, objects within the environment, speakers, and all the other bits and pieces that make up the simulation.

Performing all these tasks can slow down even the speediest computers. Unlike people, computers do not just start a task and then do it until they stop. A computer performs its actions according to the beat of an internal timer. The computer's *clock speed* regulates each step of each program that the computer is running, whether that program is a word processor or a wired-glove controller. The speed at which the computer's clock operates and the amount of work the computer can do between one *cycle*, or tick, of the clock and the next, determines whether the computer user notices any delays or other problems.

Of course, the things that the computer has to do to create the virtual environment are complicated as well. A virtual-environment's visual display is not a solid, blended mass of color, like the paint in a mural. It is made up of colored *polygons*, two-dimensional shapes with three or more sides, such as triangles and rectangles. (Strictly speaking, a circle is not a polygon, as it is a single line curved around on itself.) All landscapes and objects in VR are made up of polygons stuck next to and on top of one another. Even round objects, such as balls or columns, are made up of small polygons attached at very small angles.

Computers use up a lot of memory rendering the thousands of polygons that make up a typical virtual environment. Each line has to be plotted, colored in, shaded to represent the proper lighting effect, and adjusted for the type of stereoscopic display being used. To pres-

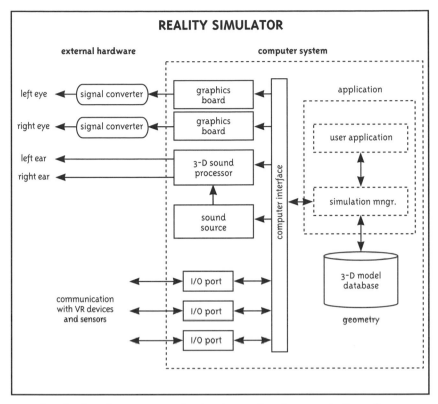

A reality simulator is a computer that has been set up to generate three-dimensional environments and coordinate user interface tools for immersive interactions.

ent virtual worlds, computers have to render and keep track of thousands of lines. Moreover, the computer constantly has to redraw each of these lines to keep them from fading from the display screen. Movements also need to be smooth and even with the user's hand or head motions; human vision is swift enough to detect delays of even a fraction of a second. The speed at which the computer redraws a scene is called the *refresh rate;* a slow refresh rate causes the display to jerk as the user moves around or alters the environment. Adding sound or touch effects places even greater burdens on the system.

Fortunately, a phenomenon of human biology called *persistence of vision* works to the advantage of virtual-environment designers. Images tend to stay in the eye for a tenth of a second after they form on the retina. This period of persistence is too fast for most people to notice, and, as fresh images normally flood the eyes every moment a person is awake, the constant stream of signals from the retina to the brain blocks out the effect. Movies, however, are made up of individual photographs of a scene that are strung together on a strip of film. So, why can people watch movies and see a smooth flow of action, rather than just a rapid series of still photos? The reason is that movies are projected fast enough—30 frames a second, or three frames every tenth of a second—for each photo to overlap the fading image of the previous one before it disappears. Because the vision centers of the brain have evolved to perceive action as a smooth flow, they automatically blend the images.

A tenth of a second may not seem like a lot of time to a person, but to a fast computer, a tenth of a second can be the equivalent of hours or days in human terms. Just as movies present a series of frames on film, computers render scenes in terms of frames per second, constantly redrawing the image as it responds to the user's actions. Over the years, computer-graphics experts have learned that rendering 10 to 12 frames a second—roughly the same speed as the average person's persistence of vision—provides an acceptable level of interaction in low-level systems, while 30 frames a second (the same speed as movies) is the fastest any system needs to perform.

Similar rules apply to the movement of a user's hand or the computer-generated figure that represents his or her body. Fortunately for computer designers, nerve signals move a little more slowly through the human body than electrons move through well-designed computer circuits. To transfer nerve signals, nerve cells squirt out chemicals that flow across their synapses (the gap between the ends of adjacent nerve cells). When a nerve receives these chemicals, it generates a small electric charge that zaps across to its opposite end, where the charge triggers another jolt of chemicals to carry the signal to the next nerve or group of nerves. In a computer's circuits, there is no need to switch between electric and chemical signals. The only factors that determine how fast the electrons flow are the length of the wires in a circuit and the number of switches, transistors, and other components in the electrons' path. With a fast enough clock speed and well-designed circuits, computers can take time to run the numbers for its virtual environment and still appear to be working instantaneously.

Computer designers and programmers use a few other hardware tricks to speed up the work of rendering worlds. *Preprocessors* are microchips or circuit boards that prepare data for computation—such as calculating the position of a user's fingers from the sensors in a wired glove—or take some of the calculation burden off the main processing circuits. Graphics cards and sound cards are two of the most commonly used preprocessors, both in regular computer systems and in reality engines.

Adding more memory also affects computer power. Memory chips are like electronic cupboards where computers put information they need to work with right away, such as the shape and color of virtual objects, or temporarily store data from programs that are running. Computers that have more memory can perform more tasks; in immersive computing, having more memory provides shorter lag times as well as greater amounts of detail in the digital environment. (Components such as hard-disk drives are not considered part of a computer's memory; they are used for long-term data storage or to store information that is not needed frequently.)

Reality Simulation Across the Internet

Another method gives people the opportunity to take part in immersive environments even if their computers are not up to the entire task of creating a virtual world. If they wish, people can visit three-dimensional domains on the Internet, one of the world-spanning networks of interconnected computers that have become international shipping routes for information. People have interacted with each other for years through *multi-user dungeons*, or MUDS, that originally were created for fantasy role-playing games. MUDs and live chat rooms are like typewritten telephone calls between many people at once, taking place strictly through text messages. Because the participants learn about each other only through the words they type on their computers, they can and do give themselves any name they wish and describe themselves any way they desire. It is up to each person to image how their surroundings and the people they interact with would look like if they all were in a physical space. (In fact, some people refer to this type of interchange as *text-based virtual reality*.)

In the 1990s, some programmers began adding pictures to the words. On-line communities that incorporated two- and three-dimensional computer graphics began springing up on the World Wide Web, the subset of the Internet that uses pictures, sound files, and clickable links to connect people to data. These visual counterparts to MUDs originally were known as MOOs, short for *multi-user dungeons, object oriented*. In such on-line worlds, participants interact with each other using *avatars*, computer-generated figures that take the place of the participant's body in the MOO. (The word *avatar* originally referred to the human or animal forms supposedly assumed by the gods of Hinduism during their visits on Earth. The term became associated with the graphical figurines, as they are the temporary embodiment of their human controllers in the computer-generated environment.)

MOOs can be enjoyable places. Participants can walk or (if the feature is programmed into the community) fly throughout the environment, be it a village, a chain of tropical islands, or a space station. In some communities, the participants can construct buildings, gardens, mountains, and other counterparts to the physical world. There are no such things as sun, wind, rain, unless they are part of the world's design. Though property lines and building codes can determine where structures are placed, virtual environments are not constrained by fire dangers, restrictions on water and sewer services, worries about budget limits, or many of the other factors of physical life. The true limits to a virtual environment are the amount of memory a computer system has, the speed at which the computer operates, and the skill of the programmer or programmers involved in building the environment.

Though each company that produces one of these on-line communities may call it by a different name, the most common term for the programming technique that makes these environments possible is *Virtual Reality Modeling Language*, or VRML (pronounced *vermal*). It is a three-dimensional counterpart to the *Hypertext Markup Language* (HTML) that allows Web users to switch from one on-screen page of information to another using transfer commands contained in icons, on-screen buttons, and highlighted words or phrases. VRML sites use two-dimensional displays and a selection of simple mouse-and-keyboard commands to create the impression that users are moving through three-dimensional environments. The effect is similar to playing a video game without the need to score points or avoid monsters.

When VRML first appeared as a computer language in the mid-1990s, many people questioned whether it really could be considered virtual reality. It was not immersive; its displays were presented inside computerized frames within the larger frame of a computer monitor. It did not allow for much interaction. There were few, if any, options for handling objects or doing similar tasks. Also, VRML worlds were notorious for taking a long time to load into a person's computer and then not working when the download was completed. Computer industry experts said that VRML would need a lot of work before it became a useful component of Internet computing.

These days, there are different methods of creating on-line three-dimensional worlds that work around these problems. The programs that run these worlds are more reliable, thanks to new programming languages and the general improvement in computer technology. Also, the amount of data that can be transmitted over the Internet, or *bandwidth*, has increased dramatically, creating a better connection between host computers and users' computers. Thus, there is a better level of interaction between participants themselves and between participants and the on-line environment. Aside from on-line communities, computer-aided design (CAD) applications, and a few other uses, though, VRML did not lead to the widespread use of 3-D graphics on the World Wide Web. (Some of the people who created and supported VRML are trying to create a new, better language for 3-D programming called Extensible 3D, or X3D, that could work on Web pages created using Extensible Markup Language, or XML.)

But the hardware that supports these environments is no good without the software that creates them. To understand what reality engines do, it is necessary to know a little bit about computer graphics.

9

GRAPHICS: POLYGONS AND PERSPECTIVES

In many ways, the computer graphics of virtual worlds are the same as those in other types of three-dimensional programs, such as some modern video games, and in strictly two-dimensional programs, such as standard on-screen desktops. Each type of program contains specific instructions on how to draw background images, where to place usable objects, and which figures represent computer users. All these programs set down rules for how various elements can and cannot interact, as well as for the results of any interactions that do occur. Other rules determine which elements players or participants can see at any moment.

A standard personal-computer desktop, for example, is a graphical interface that uses program icons, buttons, and other on-screen controls, rather than typed-in codes, to open files and work with software. Mouse-controlled pointers represent a user's hand and fingers. The desktop program also controls the display of information. When people have multiple windows open on their computers, they expect to see just the window they are working in, without having images from other windows show through. The same expectations apply to 3-D video games, which present environments that seem to exist all around the player's character, even though only a portion appears on the screen. It would look strange if a character went from a jungle landscape into a windowless building but still was able to see the jungle through the supposedly solid walls.

Computer-graphics artists have to make sure mistakes like these do not happen, especially in virtual environments. When people work with objects in a virtual environment, they expect to see those objects more or less the way they would appear in real life (unless the world is programmed to display objects in a different way). A medical student working with a virtual model of a surgery patient might expect to see the patient's internal organs through a hole cut in his or her chest, but not the floor beneath the operating table. One of the great challenges in designing realistic virtual worlds is to account for all these factors while still making the world fast enough to respond to its users.

The Starting Point for Computer Graphics

Keeping track of a virtual-world's details can be tricky because of the way computers draw and manage the environment. As mentioned in the previous chapter, computers render landscapes and objects by drawing, connecting, and coloring in huge numbers of multiple-sided polygons. Placing these polygons on a computer monitor or a head-mounted display screen is a matter of geometry, using mathematical formulas to define lines, form flat and curved surfaces, and indicate solid objects. Trying to draw each object as a single image would use up too much memory—a separate image would be required for every possible view of the object—and would slow the display almost to a standstill as the computer tried to coordinate all the images of each object.

Polygons provide a simple way to change the shape and the appearance of digital items. Because each polygon has a fixed number of lines and angles, changing the shape and the appearance of digital items simply means changing line lengths and angular measurements. Triangles are the easiest polygons to draw, but programmers often use polygons with more sides to design large objects, complex shapes, or objects that need to be flexible (such as human or animal bodies). With modern computer-graphics software, all a designer has to do is select a point on the object's surface and move it to another position. The computer instantly can calculate how to change the object's lines and angles to match up with the designer's alteration.

USING POLYGONS TO CREATE VIRTUAL ENVIRONMENTS

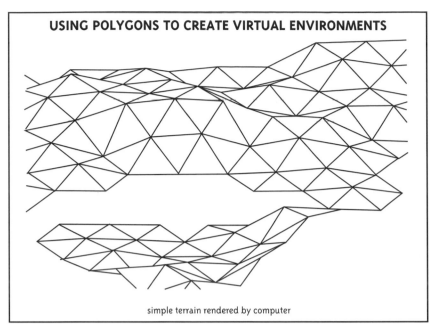

simple terrain rendered by computer

Higher polygon counts mean higher levels of detail in a virtual environment as well as higher levels of realism. Less-complex environments can be made to seem more realistic with shading techniques or by wrapping the polygons with digital designs called texture maps.

Artists begin creating computer graphics by assembling *wireframe* models of the scenes and objects they wish to construct. (These models get their name because, while they are computer images, they look like something that has been created by bending a bunch of wires into shape.) A wireframe model is the skeleton of the eventual object; it shows the connected polygons that form the image's structure, along with any other lines or curves that will provide added detail once the model is colored in. Many of the curves in computer graphics, by the way, are defined by mathematical formulas that establish how much a line bends; these curves are referred to as *splines*. Other curves are made up of many small line segments that are connected end to end at slight angles to one another; these curves are called *polylines*.

With all those polygons and all the points at which they connect, it is not unusual for something to go wrong with the display. Gaps in the surface of an environment's background image, portions of an object that seem to break off when the object is moved, lines or panels that seem to fly out from an object's side—these and other problems can pop up when polygons do not match up exactly or when unneeded lines are added accidentally. When these mistakes occur, programmers use their wireframe models to identify and correct the errors.

Once the designer finishes assembling the wireframe model, he or she can fill in the structure with colors, textures, shading effects, and other details to make the object seem more realistic. Here is another potential stumbling point in the creation of a computer environment. Rendering details such as the position and color of each brick in a wall, for example, is a task that takes a great deal of time and memory simply for a two-dimensional display. Adding the burden of rendering scenes for stereoscopic presentations can make the job even more complicated.

Computer-graphics programmers long ago figured out a way to sidestep this problem. Instead of having the computer draw in all these details from scratch, programmers use *texture maps*—small, computerized "photographs" of different materials or real-world objects that can be pasted onto any surface represented by a group of connected polygons. In a sense, using a texture map is like making prints of a painting

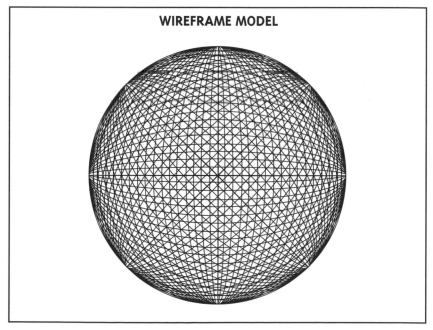

Wireframe models serve as the skeletons for objects within computer-graphics images, including virtual environments.

for use in a poster. The hardest part of the job, creating the original image, only has to be done one time by the artist. Making the posters, which are nothing more than copies of the image, is a much easier process.

The instructions for creating the surface of a wall would read something like this (if translated from computer code into English): "After drawing the outline of the wall, copy the image in the file 'wall one' onto the wall's surface, starting from the left edge and stopping at the right edge." With all the segments of the wall covered in copies of the texture file, the wall would appear as an even, unbroken surface. The only task left for the software to do would be to adjust the shade of the texture maps to harmonize with the rest of the environment.

Making a Virtual Scene Come "Alive"

In a movie or a television program, the position of the cameras determines what images will appear in the theater or on a TV screen. In fact, one of the first things directors decide is how the final version of the movie or show will appear. They create a storyboard, a series of drawings that show how each scene will look, and then figure out later where to place their cameras to record that scene. During filming, they make sure their sets are in the right shape, and that the actors are positioned correctly, when the cameras start recording. A piece of studio equipment (like an overhead microphone) that comes within the camera's field of view, or an actor standing outside the field, can interfere with the connection between the audience and the show.

A similar principle applies to creating virtual environments. Because the cameras of a virtual world, eventually, are the users' eyes, virtual-world designers have to make sure their environments look right from every angle that a user might see them. The software they use helps them with this task, by providing virtual cameras that can display scenes from different angles at the same time and virtual spotlights that can illuminate the environment from any position. As they build the world and place objects within it, the designers also perform a series of virtual walk-throughs to gain a first-hand perspective on how the world is shaping up.

As much as it means figuring out what should be shown, the goal of making environments look right also means identifying details that

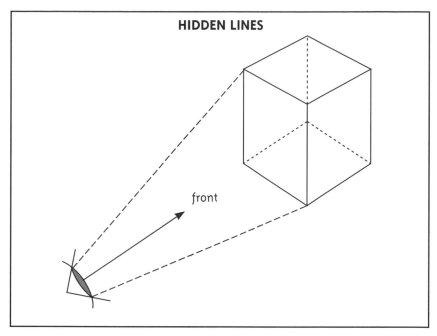

HIDDEN LINES

front

Someone looking at a solid, three-dimensional object can see only those surfaces and edges closest to his or her eyes. To create a successful illusion of depth and immersion in a 3-D space, virtual environments have to provide similar perceptive cues by erasing or hiding lines and surfaces that a user should not see. For instance, a VR user looking at a cube (above) would be able to see its front, top, and right sides; the edges represented by the dashed lines and the bottom, left, and rear sides would either not be drawn or would be masked by the visible portions of the cube.

should not be shown. When people look at the front of a building, they do not see lines representing the shape of the building's sides or rear. The front of the building hides the rest of the structure from view, just as any solid object can block the view of any other object. This does not happen automatically with a computer-graphics display: Unless the computer is told otherwise, it will render all of the lines of an object, front and back, at the same time. To make sure that the only visible lines are ones that should be seen, programmers have to identify *hidden lines* that the computer should not draw when it renders a scene. Fortunately, modern computer-graphics software simplifies this part of the job by automatically defining where polygons overlap, calculating which polygons are closest to the user's eyes, and determining which lines to leave out.

Virtual-environment designers also have to make sure they are designing their worlds with the proper perspective. In the real world, distant objects appear smaller than objects that are close to hand. If an environment is supposed to behave like the real world, closer objects have to appear larger than distant ones, and all objects have to change in size as the user moves around. Once again, commercially produced graphics software packages include features that help programmers take care of details such as these.

Obviously, an environment can produce a better sense of reality if it does not have a lot of details to render in the first place. Depending on how fast and powerful its reality engine is, an environment with a high *polygon count*—the total number of polygons in every object in the environment—can take much longer to put together than one with fewer polygons. If the delay in rendering changes to the environment is long enough, it can interfere with the sense of immersion in the virtual world. A less-complex environment can appear blocky and cartoonish, but researchers who have built seemingly simplistic worlds have found they can achieve surprisingly effective levels of immersion, especially among average people who are not computer-programming experts.

Other factors that virtual-world designers have to incorporate in their graphic displays include the phenomena of *collision detection* and lighting. In computer graphics, the word *collision* does not mean a forceful crash, but merely the interaction of one solid object with another when each one tries to occupy the same space. When a bird lands on a branch, its feet rest on the branch's surface. In graphics terms, that contact is a collision, because the surface of the bird's feet has collided with the surface of the branch. Likewise, a leaf blowing through the air will stop when it collides with the side of a house.

In a computer-graphics display, the leaf could pass through the side of the house if there are no instructions telling it to stop. Proper collision detection instructions keep objects from passing through each other. Collision detection also can trigger responses to these interactions, such as a window breaking when hit by a flying ball or a cup bouncing when it drops on a tabletop.

When people talk about lighting in computer graphics, they are referring to the use of color and shading techniques to re-create the effects light has in the real world. Computer graphics themselves do not need to be illuminated, of course, as display screens provide their own light (except for some liquid-crystal displays, which require backlights for their images to be seen). However, images with no highlights or shadows look flat and unrealistic, while scenes in which all the objects

RADIOSITY

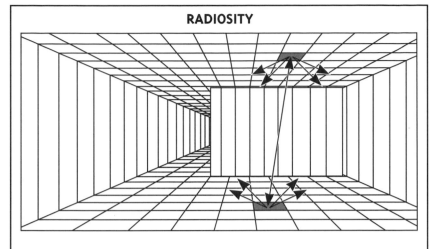

- Radiosity assumes every polygon will give off some light
- Radiosity is good at diffuse reflections over object surfaces

RAY TRACING

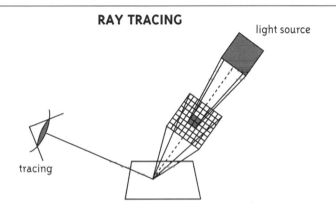

light source

tracing

- Ray tracing calculates the path that light would follow from viewer's eye to object, then from object to any light source
- Ray tracing is represented by line from viewer's eye to the large surface and by dotted line from surface to small light source
- Ray tracing provides mirrorlike reflections

Ray tracing and radiosity are two methods used to determine lighting within a computer-graphics image. With ray tracing, computer artists trace a path from the viewer's eye to objects he or she would be able to see, then determine how bright and detailed that object would appear under the lighting conditions of its environment. Radiosity is a method for reproducing more diffuse lighting effects: Designers assume each polygon in an image is a light source of its own and compute how these sources would enhance and interfere with one another, creating softer lighting and shadow effects. These and other effects can be combined in creating images and environments.

appear to be illuminated exactly the same way appear equally artificial. Computer-graphics artists compensate for these details by making colors lighter or darker, changing the amount of detail that surfaces display, and altering the way shadows look. They also can incorporate small programs that imitate the effect of daylight, table lamps, candles, flashlights, or other light sources within the environment.

One of the many methods of re-creating lighting effects in computer graphics is called *ray tracing*. In ray tracing, the computer first calculates where the viewer is looking and what portions of the environment might fall within his or her line of sight. Then, the computer traces a path from the viewer's eyes to each portion of the environment, essentially going backward along the path that light rays would take from the objects to the eyes. Once the computer works out what the viewer might see, it traces the path from the objects to any "light source" within the scene, again following the path that light would take from its source to the rest of the environment. This way, the computer determines if an object would be illuminated by a real light source in such a way that the viewer would see that object. From then on, the computer will render the object with the appropriate amount of color, texture, and shading, keeping track of the viewer's actions and making any changes to the scene.

Coordinating Virtual Worlds

Making objects and environments look right is a big part of creating virtual worlds. Another big part of the job is making sure these items interact correctly with one another and with people who work within the digitized domain. As mentioned earlier, collision detection keeps objects from passing through each other, just as hidden-line detection keeps the images of objects from appearing within figures that supposedly are in front of them. But what is it that enforces these and other rules as a person is moving through a virtual world?

In general, the referee of a virtual world is a piece of software called a *simulation manager*. Like operating systems that regulate how various components in a personal computer work with one another, the simulation manager tells the computer how to coordinate input from the user with the interactions of objects in the digitized environment. It performs this feat by making the computer run through a sequence of actions called a *simulation event loop* many times a second. During each repetition of the loop, the computer will establish what actions the user has performed; where the user has moved in the environment, where objects in

Combining a few basic textures and elements can yield a highly useful environment. Here, a few computer-generated shapes and textures are combined to form part of a river navigation training system. [Image courtesy: VR Mariner]

the environment need to be placed; and what actions, if any, the environment needs to take in response to the user (for example, opening an automatic door as the user approaches it). Finally, the simulation manager will order the computer to render images, as well as play any sounds or generate any textures, in response to these interactions.

Just as reality engines can have special circuit cards that make these tasks easier to perform, simulation designers use programming techniques to reduce the amount of work the computers have to do. One of the most common techniques is to handle complex tasks or operations that need to be performed over and over using mathematical equations called *algorithms*.

For example, imagine that someone wants to create a computer-graphics display showing what it would look like to dump a box of table tennis balls on the floor. It would take too much time to plot a course each ball would follow as it hits the floor and bounces away. Instead, the programmer would use an algorithm to figure out each ball's path independently, starting from the ball's position as it falls out of the box and recalculating the path as the ball bounces against the floor, a wall, and other Ping-Pong balls. Even with a large number of Ping-Pong balls, running an algorithm is a fast enough method to create the display in real time.

Algorithms often are used to create landscapes and other features that otherwise would have to be designed polygon by polygon. A type of algorithm called a *fractal algorithm* uses an advanced form of geometry to create shapes that resemble those found in nature, such as the patterns within a row of hills or the appearance of a tree full of leaves.

DISPLAYS: LOOKING AND LISTENING IN VR

For the majority of people, sight is the most important sense they have for dealing with the physical world. People generally get most of their information through their eyes: where they are, what things are around them, how far away those things are, and so forth. The other four senses mainly help to clarify or reinforce the signals that the eyes send to the brain. In fact, people often do not learn how much information they can gather about the world with their hearing, their sense of touch, and their senses of smell and taste unless they lose their vision or are born without the ability to see.

Much of the work that goes into creating a virtual environment centers on the need to make it look right, and not just to create the visual sense of immersion in the digital world. When visitors to a virtual world believe what their eyes seem to be showing them is real, then it is easier to create audio, tactile, and other sensations that seem to be real as well. In fact, people often begin to experience a sense of movement when watching a realistic, fast-moving scene on a large, two-dimensional display like a movie screen or a big-screen television. This feeling may come from the fact that the brain expects to detect a type of motion when it perceives that certain types of action are under way. The false sense of movement may be the result of the brain's anticipation that it will soon be receiving those signals as well as the visual ones.

In the real world, touch is the second-most-used sense after sight, with hearing coming in third. In digitized environments, however, it is easier to create the sense of sound and to build sophisticated speakers than it is to generate computerized textures and create the tools to detect them. And, as the ears and the eyes are so conveniently located at the same level on the head, many VR visual displays contain or support *stereophonic* speakers as well. Together, the two types of display can give users a lot of the information they need to accept the virtual environment as real.

Virtual Visualization

As mentioned earlier, mimicking three-dimensional, or *stereoscopic*, sight is a matter of presenting slightly different views of an image to each eye. The brain overlaps and blends these images in its *optic lobes*, creating the illusion of physical depth in the environment. The trick to successfully deceiving the brain this way—as Sir David Brewster found with his improved stereoscope—is to place these images close enough together, and near enough to the eyes, for the blending effect to occur.

Beginning with Ivan Sutherland's work in the 1960s, the most direct way to display three-dimensional computer environments is through a head-mounted display, or HMD. When properly adjusted, HMDs present images at just the right distance from the eyes for easy viewing and at exactly the right distance between each other to create stereo vision. In fact, the type of display that Sutherland developed for the Sword of Damocles—two cathode-ray tubes whose images are reflected into the user's eyes—still is used to provide clear, sharp images of virtual worlds.

Modern cathode-ray tube HMDs work much like the Sword or the VCASS/SuperCockpit helmet that Tom Furness and his air force research team developed. A cathode-ray tube hangs on each side of the user's head, with the display screen pointing forward. Like television picture tubes, the tiny CRTs use tight beams of electrons to paint scenes and objects on the inside surface of the screen. An arrangement of mirrors or optical prisms (which can bend or reflect light) transmits the image from the CRT into the user's eyes. HMDs that use cathode-ray tubes give a sharper, clearer picture than do most LCD screens.

There are a few drawbacks to the cathode-ray design. First, making tubes that small is an expensive process, and the final product can be

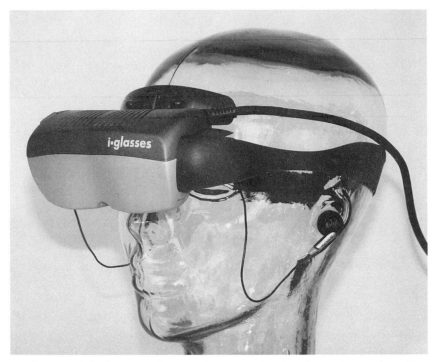

Head-mounted displays come in many shapes, ranging from large visors such as this one to smaller units shaped like large sunglasses. [Image courtesy: I-O Display Systems]

among the most expensive bits of VR hardware on the market. The better picture comes at other costs as well. The tubes are heavier than other types of viewers, and using a CRT display for a long time can pose neck and back problems. CRTs also can be much riskier to use because they place powerful electric currents next to the user's head.

Liquid-crystal head-mounted displays solve many of these problems, but create a few others in the process. These HMDs are the viewers people usually think of first when they think of virtual reality or immersive-environment technology. They all are descendants of the type that Mike McGreevy developed for VIVED and Scott Fisher incorporated in VIEW. Most liquid-crystal HMDs use separate display screens for each eye, combined with lenses that make the picture seem larger and prevent users from straining to focus on the picture.

Each square screen measures a couple of inches across and connects either to its own group of microchips within the reality simulator. Each screen gets its own set of controllers because each screen has to display a slightly different view of the same scene. As remarkable as micro-processors are these days, they still can only do one job at a time, and trying to use the same chips to run each screen would make the images flicker. Some less-expensive HMDs, which people use when they do not need a stereographic display, have only one *monoscopic*, or single-view, screen connected to a single graphics board.

Using a liquid-crystal HMD has had a few drawbacks. For most of the 1990s, LCDs were not capable of displaying images with the same *resolution*, or amount of detail, that cathode-ray tubes could provide. At the end of the 1990s and the beginning of the 2000s, LCD monitors were much better, though they still were not as crisp and clear as CRTs. Also, LCD pictures can be hard to see when they have to compete with open lighting, so it is all but impossible to reflect an LCD image into the eyes with lenses that would allow people to see the real world at the same time. Solutions to this problem have included building HMDs with swing-up visors that contain the picture screens. This way, users can take a break from their virtual environments and interact with the real world without having to remove the headset.

A different type of display incorporates the optics of the HMD in a separate housing that people hold in front of their eyes, rather than wearing it like a helmet. One of the first of these displays, the Binocular Omni-Orientation Monitor by Fake Space Labs (now called Fakespace Systems), mounted its viewer on a swinging arm that tracked where the user's eyes were pointing. More recently, some companies have developed a display shaped like a pair of binoculars with a built-in position tracker.

"Sunglasses" for the VR World

Sometimes it is either too expensive or too impractical to use fully immersive head-mounted displays for three-dimensional viewing. In such cases, it is possible to create 3-D images with two-dimensional computer monitors, much as filmmakers of the 1950s created them on movie screens. There are a few ways to accomplish this feat.

One method uses roughly the same type of gimmick as those used to create the illusion of depth in 3-D movies—a set of glasses with a different kind of lens for each eye. Each lens may be a different color, such as red and blue, or they may have a different polarity, allowing some light beams through and blocking others. Whichever way the glasses

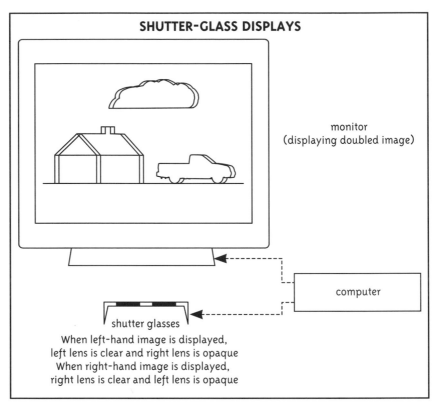

SHUTTER-GLASS DISPLAYS

monitor
(displaying doubled image)

computer

shutter glasses
When left-hand image is displayed,
left lens is clear and right lens is opaque
When right-hand image is displayed,
right lens is clear and left lens is opaque

Shutter-glass displays provide the illusion of depth to images displayed on two-dimensional screens, such as a standard computer monitor or the wall of a CAVE. The VR computer sends two images of the virtual environment to the screen, one giving a left-eye view and the other giving a right-eye view. Shifting very rapidly between the two views, the computer creates the appearance that it is displaying a single doubled image. At the same time, the computer darkens and clears each lens of the shutter glasses in sync with the shift from one image to the other. Each eye sees only one image of the scene; the brain blends these images, creating the illusion of stereoscopic vision.

are made, the VR system renders two images on the monitor at the same time; each lens blocks out one of the images, giving each eye a separate view to send to the brain. Combined in the visual cortex, the two views will yield a seeming three-dimensional image. Sometimes, these glasses will be the same cardboard-and-plastic-film type that magazines include in special 3-D issues or that people get on three-dimensional motion rides. However, some displays use higher-quality glasses, with plastic frames and larger, more durable lenses that are meant to last.

Another method uses glasses with a type of liquid-crystal lens that either lets all light through or blocks out all light, like a shutter on a window. These lenses work like the lenses of light-sensitive sunglasses, which automatically darken when exposed to sunlight, only they work much faster and are triggered by electric currents. Separate lenses over each eye alternately block one eye and then the other from seeing the computer monitor. At the same time, the computer displays alternating left eye/right eye views of the virtual environment. The display and the lenses of the shutter glasses operate in sync, switching views at least 30 times each second.

Shutter glasses have been a part of PC-based virtual reality kits, usually ones that allow people to play three-dimensional combat and driving games, and of more advanced systems that are devoted to scientific research and computer-assisted design work. But, as with other types of display, the glasses have some limitations. They also provide a little more desk clutter, connecting with a wire to a circuit board in the computer that powers the lenses and coordinates their shutter effect

Combined with special graphics methods, shutter glasses turn flat-panel screens into three-dimensional displays. [Courtesy NASA [Ames Research Center]]

with the on-screen display. The glasses also may have their own batteries, rather than draw power from the computer, and thus will be a bit heavy or cumbersome to wear.

A third type of glasses display uses LCD screens to provide a monoscopic view for people who want to use their computer without using a large monitor or when they want to watch a movie on a portable DVD player. Though they do not provide a sense of depth or immersion in a world of data, they give the impression of having a large-screen display suspended a few feet in front of the user's head.

Stereoscopic Displays for the Bare Eye

A few stereoscopic displays can mimic the depth and appearance of the physical world without requiring viewers to wear headsets, glasses, or any other cumbersome device. One of these displays places a large liquid-crystal display in front of a series of narrow light panels. The LCD screen displays the left-eye and right-eye images at different angles, switching rapidly between the two to prevent each eye from seeing the opposite image. This *autostereoscopic*, or self-contained 3-D, method has one severe drawback: The illusion of depth takes place only if the user is looking directly at the screen. Any movement beyond a very narrow limit destroys the illusion. Other types of stand-alone stereovisions let the image follow the viewer's eye using a series of long, vertical prisms in front of the display screen. As the viewer changes position, he or she sees the image from another set of facets, which are designed to show the proper left or right view of the scene to the correct eye.

Advanced air force flight simulators and some VR video game companies use a third type of successful and nonobtrusive 3-D display. This system uses a series of lenses and computer graphics tricks to fool the eyes into focusing beyond the surface of the computer screen. This arrangement gives an illusion of depth similar to that offered by HMDs or shutter glasses but with much clearer pictures.

Three-dimensional Sound

For all the diversity of methods for showing virtual worlds, there are not yet very many different ways of creating three-dimensional sound.

People hear in three dimensions much as they see in three dimensions, by overlapping two separate sets of signals. Our ears detect *sound waves*, which are nothing more than vibrations that travel through the air. Actions—someone tapping a pencil against a book, a rock rolling downhill, a bird chirping—knock air molecules together, creating a little shock wave that spreads out from the object or the action that made the sound. We interpret these shock waves as sound by the effect they have on the tiny structures within our ears: the eardrum, which the sound waves strike first; the bones of the middle ear, which vibrate in response to the vibrations of the eardrum; and the cochlea, which contain sensory cells that pick up the vibrations from the middle ear and send signals to the brain.

The ability to hear *spatial sound*—to tell where sounds are coming from—comes from the difference in the way each ear captures a particular set of sound waves. For example, imagine walking down a sidewalk when a nearby car blows out a tire. Three things happen. First,

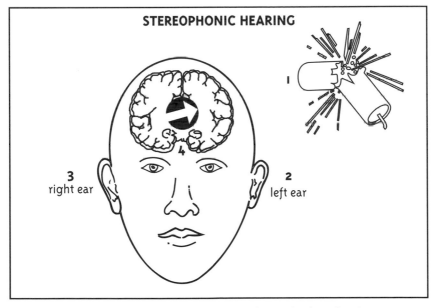

STEREOPHONIC HEARING

3
right ear

2
left ear

Like stereoscopic vision, stereophonic hearing is the result of overlapping two sets of signals in the brain. Sound waves from a sound source (1) reach one ear (2) more rapidly and with slightly greater intensity than they reach the other (3). The hearing centers of the brain combine the two signals sent by the ears and determine the direction of the sound's source (4).

the sound of the blowout reaches the ear closer to the car a split second before it gets to the other ear. Though sound waves travel at roughly 1,088 mph at sea level (and a little slower at higher elevations), human beings can perceive lags of as little as 70 microseconds, or 70 millionths of one second. This time lag is called the *interaural* ("between the ears") *time difference.*

At the same time, the sound waves strike the closer ear more forcefully than they hit the farther ear. Thus, the closer ear, which points toward the car, hears a louder version of the blowout than does the farther ear, which points away from the car. Because volume depends on a sound wave's *amplitude,* the amount of disturbance a sound wave causes in the air, the difference in volume is called the *interaural amplitude difference.*

Finally, each ear hears a different *frequency,* or range of tones, coming from the blowout. The difference depends on how much sound reflects from nearby walls, the street, and other objects. It also depends on how the sound waves bend as they travel around the listener's head to the farther ear, an effect referred to as the head-related transfer function. The brain takes all these variables and combines them to determine from which direction the sound of the blowout came.

All these factors—amplitude, time delay, differences in frequency—make creating sounds for a virtual environment more difficult than simply sticking a stereo system onto a big-screen television. For one thing, the sense of hearing is far less forgiving of mistakes and delays than is the sense of sight. The eyes and the visual cortex fill in the gaps when vision is interrupted. This ability, called *persistence of vision,* explains why people can watch a movie's rapid succession of still photos and perceive a continuous, smooth flow of action. But the ears are more sensitive to interruptions, even those as little as 70 microseconds long. Even slight breaks or quavers in a virtual-sound display can spoil the sense of immersion.

Many virtual-reality systems get around the problem by playing prerecorded sound files rather than by custom-generating sounds. A set of microphones arranged to pick up sound waves much as the human ears do records sounds in these files. Stereo music recordings are made using this method as well; in fact, much of the sound reproduction in computer systems comes from knowledge gained in the recording industry. Using stereo headphones or setting up a pattern of loudspeakers can re-create the effect of being immersed in sound.

In general, headphones provide a better sense of sonic immersion. Just as special circuit boards can adjust the visual displays for each eye, audio circuit boards can adjust the playback for each ear. For example, a person wearing a sight-and-sound HMD and standing in the middle of a virtual room might hear the sound of a radio off to one side. When that person turns to look at the radio, the sound will follow his or head around until it seems to be coming from in front of his or her head, where the radio is.

MANIPULATORS: GLOVES, WANDS, AND TRACKERS

Being able to see and hear is only part of the goal in interacting with virtual environments. If a visitor or researcher cannot travel around in and interact with the display, he or she becomes little more than a digital statue, a spectator in what should be a realm of activity. The people who created the tools of virtual reality were trying to find a way to make working with computer data as easy as working with physical objects. Working with physical objects means picking them up, moving them around, building things with them, or throwing them away. Likewise, for a virtual world to work, people have to be able to change some or all of the objects they find there, whether through adding a new building in an on-line community or turning a molecule around to examine its structure in a chemistry simulation.

In the real world, however, people perform these tasks pretty much automatically. They do not have to spend a lot of time figuring out where they are and which way they are moving. They do not have to decide where their hands are, for instance, before they reach out for a box or wait until they verify that their hands are gripping the sides of the box before they lift it. These sensations take place automatically, through a mixture of nerve signals and common sense. In a virtual environment, a series of tools and position trackers provide the data computers need to mimic these effects and figure out where each user is.

Touching Objects in Thin Air

In the first decade or so of virtual reality's existence, researchers and inventors came up with many different tools that gave people the ability to move objects and to feel the objects that they grasped. Some of these devices caught on and became part of the standard tool kit of immersive computing. Others proved to be impractical or simply too hard to use, and companies stopped making them. Today, four general types of devices allow people to manipulate objects in digital environments: wired gloves, control wands, joystick or mouse-based controllers, and haptic devices that provide a sense of touch in the virtual world.

WIRED GLOVES

Second only to head-mounted displays, the wired glove became one of the most-recognized symbols of virtual reality. Generally, it is a thin fabric glove that has a series of sensors that measure how much the hand and fingers flex. Wired gloves captured the interest of VR users mainly because they are simple to use. All users have to do to work with a glove is put it on; at most, they may need to learn a few finger gestures to control their actions, such as pointing with a finger to or in the direction they want to move. Gloves also are combined with position-tracking sensors to monitor how the user's hand moves in physical and in computer space. Controlling software lets the computer determine when the user's hand grasps an object or is blocked by an impermeable surface, like a wall.

The first commercial wired glove, the DataGlove built by VPL Research in the mid-1980s, used loops of light-conducting tubes that ran up the back of the hand and over the top of each knuckle. As the user bent his or her fingers, the tubes would pinch shut, reducing the amount of light that flowed from a tiny bulb at one end of the tube to a sensor at the other end. The computer would calculate how far the fingers had to bend to reduce the light, and then adjust the image of the user's digital hand. Some wired gloves still use light to measure how far fingers flex, though fiber optics long ago replaced light tubes, which

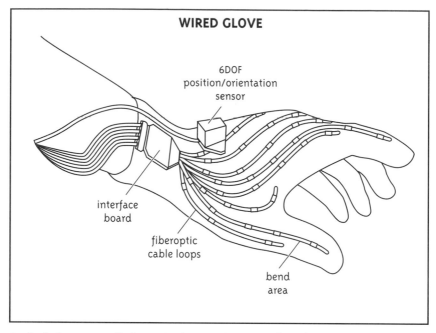

WIRED GLOVE

6DOF
position/orientation
sensor

interface
board

fiberoptic
cable loops

bend
area

A wired glove generally has a six-degree-of-freedom (6DOF) magnetic sensor to place the user's hand within a virtual environment. Fiber optics measure how far the fingers and wrist bend. Collision detection algorithms in the virtual environment determine when the hand is grasping an object or activating controls.

were not as efficient as transmitting light. Rather than pinching shut, the fiber-optic loops allow small amounts of light to escape through their sides as the finger joints bend.

Mechanical sensors are the most accurate means of measuring hand and finger movement, but they also are the most cumbersome. A mechanical glove is actually a hand-shaped framework of metal, plastic, and electrical wires that has to be strapped onto each section of the fingers and around the wrist. This *exoskeletal* glove moves as the user's fingers move, determining exactly how much each joint flexes and sending this data to the computer. This method gives the most direct connection between the user's hand and its on-screen counterpart, but it can be uncomfortable as well as expensive.

Computer animators and game programmers have adapted mechanical tracking techniques to their business as well. They use or hire people to use frameworks that look like full-body versions of the mechanical wired glove. Like the gloves, these suits have to be strapped to the arms, legs, torso, and head. Once the suits are in place, the people who are wearing them can control the movement of a computerized on-screen figure.

A few other wired gloves gather information on hand and finger movement by measuring the strength of a small electric current running through a thin tape. Twisting or bending the tape alters its *resistance* to electrons as they pass through it, changing how fast the current flows from one end to the other. Sensors monitor and report these tiny changes in speed to a control card, which works out how far the tape must have been bent. One of the earliest resistance trackers was the Mattel PowerGlove, a game controller that the Mattel toy company built in 1989 for use with the Nintendo Entertainment System. For its flex sensors, the glove used plastic strips that were painted with a type of ink that conducts electricity. It was not nearly as accurate as a fiber-optic glove, but it was accurate enough so that people bought Power-Gloves to use in experimental or home-based VR systems. Since that time, other companies have improved on this design.

WANDS

Wands can look like remote TV controls, flattened flashlights, or the handgrip of a fighter-plane joystick. Whatever their shape, control wands contain built-in position sensors and feature a set of buttons, switches, or other controllers for interacting with the environment. Wands often are part of large-scale VR displays in which a group of people needs to collaborate in a virtual environment. Under these conditions, having many people reaching out with wired gloves might make it difficult to work. Wands, however, are easy to pass from one person to another.

Wands also can be easier to incorporate into a virtual-environment display system. Wired gloves require computers to calculate the position of each finger as well as keep track of where the entire hand is moving. Wands generally have only one position sensor, which reduces the amount of work the computer has to do.

THREE-DIMENSIONAL MICE
AND SIMILAR TOOLS

The mouse did more to personalize the desktop computer than did any other *peripheral* device. People have been using mice and their point-and-click buttons to control computers ever since the original Apple

Macintosh computer went on sale in 1984 (and even earlier, with a few experimental systems). Over the years, some companies developed mice that were able to work in three dimensions, giving up-and-down controls along with the normal left-right and forward-back movements. Mice like these could be used along with or instead of wired gloves.

Usually, a 3-D mouse has a knob or a similar control that slides and tilts above a solid base, rather than rolling on balls or using optical sensors to sense movement. Sliding the knob forward, back, and from side to side controls horizontal movement in the virtual world; tilting the knob controls vertical motion. At one time, a few companies made 3-D mice that looked like their normal 2-D counterparts but included position-sensing equipment such as ultrasonic transducers and detectors. These devices did not gain much of a following, however, and eventually went off the market.

Force balls are somewhat similar to 3-D mice and are a part of some three-dimensional computer-aided design, or CAD, systems. A typical force ball looks like a rubber ball or hockey puck mounted on a platform that is connected to the computer. Pushing, pulling, and twisting the ball activates strain sensors that translate the forces into *six-degree-of-freedom (6DOF)* movement in the computer. The platform can include anywhere from two to nine buttons, which give users the ability to select, grab, and move objects or simply to change positions in the environment.

HAPTICS

Some controllers, including a few types of wired gloves, give their users a sense of how the virtual environments feel. These controllers are generally called *haptic*, or touch-sensation, devices. One type of haptic device, which can be placed in a glove or on a control handle, stimulates nerve cells in the skin to indicate textures or forces. Some of the techniques these devices use include air sacs that inflate over sensitive areas of the fingers and the palm, pins that press lightly on the tips of the fingers, and vibrators that change speed to indicate hard or soft surfaces. The SuperCockpit program of the mid-1980s used a glove with electrically sensitive quartz crystals that pressed against the pilot's fingertips to indicate he was pressing a button.

The other class of haptic device uses the method of *force-feedback*, with motors that resist or push against the user's actions. The first experiment with force-feedback computing was the GROPE-II system developed at the University of North Carolina at Chapel Hill in the early 1970s. Its developers used a modified remote manipulator arm—a ceiling-mounted mechanical tool used to operate robotic arms from a safe distance—to grasp, move, and stack virtual building blocks on a computer display. A later version, GROPE-III, used better computers to generate 3-D models of molecules that researchers could grab and stick together. Motors on the arm would resist these efforts if the molecules were not compatible.

This and other force-feedback systems required the user to stay in one place for a long time or contort their limbs in uncomfortable ways. However, in 1990, Thomas Massie, a student working at MIT's Artificial Intelligence Laboratory, developed a way to present force-feedback in a small, easily used unit. Called the PHANTOM, the device features a small jointed arm that ends in a handle shaped like a paintbrush, a free-moving thimble, or some other control. Motors at the other end of the arm apply varying levels of force in three dimensions,

Using force-feedback haptic tools, such as the PHANTOM device by SensAble Technologies, designers can sculpt computer-graphic objects like they could sculpt a clay model. [SensAble Technologies]

based on the type of surfaces or objects programmed into the virtual environment.

Writing with a pencil or pushing a button involves concentrating a force on a single point. Likewise, manipulating virtual objects with the PHANTOM involves using a single point—for example, the thimble—to transmit force from the motors to the user's muscles. Essentially, the PHANTOM tricks the brain into perceiving the pressure against the muscles as evidence of solid shapes or different textures.

Other types of force-feedback controllers use exoskeletal frameworks that encase a hand or arm, with various sizes of motors to supply the resistance, or provide less-complicated handles for their users. In recent years, companies that make peripheral devices for home computers have been incorporating force-feedback techniques into some of their products. Joysticks that shake, vibrate, or push back against their users' hands give added levels of control and interaction with combat and sports-action games, while force-feedback driving wheels do the same for racing and off-road games. In the past, some computer accessory companies have built computer mice that provide touch effects when a computer pointer rolls over an on-screen button, a section of hypertext on a World Wide Web page, or a similar feature. Among other things, this feature supposedly made it easier for people select buttons or other on-screen features.

Keeping Track of Where You Are

Of course, people can grab hold of virtual objects only if they can get close enough to touch them. For a virtual world to be of any use to its participants, it has to be able to find out where they are and what they are doing. This is where *trackers* come in. Trackers are position-sensing devices that translate a person's real-world movements into data. Unlike the sensors on the fingers of wired gloves, which measure just the short-range motion of the fingers, trackers follow the movement of an entire hand or body through space. The computers use this data to calculate the user's position in and movement through the space of the virtual environment.

The best trackers are those that offer six-degree-of-freedom movement. Computer-graphic displays are organized along the *Cartesian coordinate system*, which divides space into three *axes:* the X axis, which tracks left-right movement; the Y axis, which tracks up-down movement; and the Z axis, which tracks forward-backward movement. Things can move along these axes or twist around them. Each type of movement is considered a separate degree of freedom. A 6DOF device monitors and responds to any movement in any of the three Cartesian axes. In contrast, a *three-degree-of-freedom (3DOF)* device might monitor movement along these axes but not around them.

There are five types of trackers being used in VR systems right now:

Magnetic trackers   These are the type of trackers that MIT researchers used in "Put That There" and that were a part of the VCASS/SuperCockpit helmet and the NASA VIEW projects. The heart of the magnetic tracking system is a small sensor that

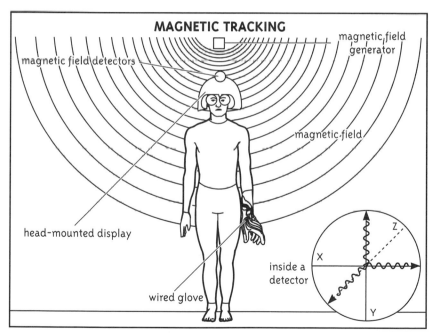

Magnetic tracking systems combine a magnetic field generator, often mounted on a ceiling, with one or more detecting units that measure how far they are from the generator. Three coiled wires inside the detectors are mounted at right angles to one another along the X, Y, and Z Cartesian axes. This arrangement provides the data needed to fix the detector's position in three dimensions and to determine which way the unit—and the effector, such as a head-mounted display or a wired glove, to which the unit is attached—is facing.

can be attached to almost any object or surface. For some applications, such as tracking the position of a wand, one sensor is enough. More sensors are needed for tracking larger objects that take up a lot of space, such as a human body.

The sensors detect the strength of magnetic fields created by small field generators that have to be placed nearby. The closer they are to the generator, the stronger the signal. A control box receives data from the sensors and determines their position in the magnetic field. Magnetic tracking is the easiest and most economical method of tracking movement, and thus the one most commonly used in VR systems. However, it also is vulnerable to interference: Unshielded metallic objects within the field can distort the sensors' readings.

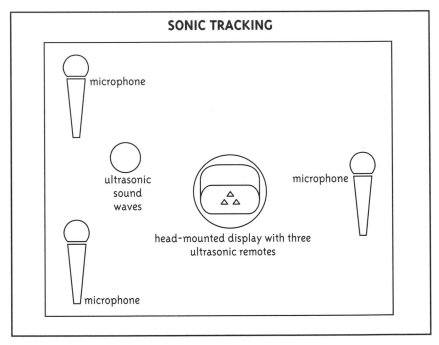

SONIC TRACKING

microphone

ultrasonic
sound
waves

microphone

head-mounted display with three
ultrasonic remotes

microphone

Sonic tracking systems use ultrasonic pulses to determine position and movement. In the type of system pictured above, three microphones mounted around a workspace pick up signals from three emitters mounted on a user's HMD. The delay between the time the speakers send out ultrasound pulses (each at a different frequency) and the time each microphone detects the pulses lets the system determine where the speakers, and the effectors to which they are mounted, are in the room.

VR displays and controllers can take many shapes. This display has been built in the shape of a pair of binoculars. [Image courtesy: n-Vision Incorporated]

Ultrasonic trackers Like magnetic trackers, ultrasonic trackers use body-mounted sensors to pick up signals generated by a fixed source. In this case, the sensors are tiny microphones that pick up ultrasonic pulses sent out by three *transducers*, devices that change electric pulses into sound waves. The transducers usually are mounted at the points of a triangle on a ceiling or overhead framework; this way, the signals they emit can cover as large an area as possible. Ultrasonic tracking systems use at least three microphones to detect the transducers' signals and compare the time it takes each signal to reach each microphone.

An ultrasonic tracker can provide very precise measurements of head, arm, and body position. The main problem that people who use these trackers run into is having sound waves bounced toward or away from the microphone by objects such as boxes, desks, or cabinets.

Gyroscopic or inertial trackers These trackers use very small gyroscopes to tell which way a user is tilting his or her head, hands, or body. Inertial trackers are not very common in current VR systems because they are not truly six-degree-of-freedom devices. They only measure changes in orientation, not changes in position. They can tell if a person moves his or her head left or right, but not if that person walks across a room.

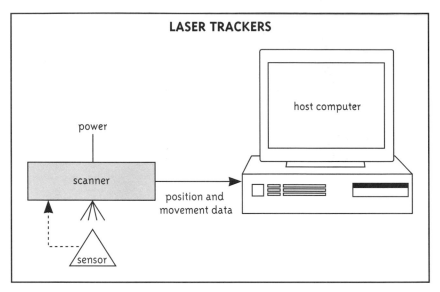

LASER TRACKERS

host computer

power

scanner

position and
movement data

sensor

Like magnetic tracking systems, laser trackers use sensors to pick up signals sent out by transmitters that are attached to reality simulators.

Mechanical trackers   Ivan Sutherland's Sword of Damocles display, which used a pivoting metal post to track the direction the person wearing the HMD was looking, was the first mechanical tracker used as part of a computer-generated environment display. Most mechanical trackers can be used only if the user sits or stands in one place, or if the user is willing to work within the space that a mechanical arm can reach.

Visual trackers   This system uses video monitors to track light-emitting diodes (LEDs) or special reflective targets placed on the user. In VR systems, such targets usually only need to be on a head-mounted display. Visual trackers are very expensive, though, enough so that they are used only in highly advanced and highly expensive immersive-environment systems such as flight simulators. In computer animation and special-effects work, on the other hand, visual tracking is the most efficient and least expensive way to create characters that move realistically. Actors, dancers, and stunt performers who are covered with dozens of targets often will spend hours performing scenes and movements on a small stage to give animators the motion data they need.

12

THE LARGER VIEW: CAVEs, WALLS, AND DESKS

During the early days of virtual reality, people noticed that head-mounted displays and other effectors put limits on how well large groups could experience digital environments. Getting the display and the tools up and running was not too difficult if there were just a few participants at a time. However, trying to bring in more people put too much stress on the reality simulators and their attached effectors. Too many participants caused the system to slow down or crash to a stop as it tried to coordinate all the different sensors and displays.

Of course, a few people could put on the VR equipment, explore the environment, and then pass the gear to others in the group. This solution caused other problems, however. Even if the "newcomers" already knew how to move through the environment, they had to orient themselves to the display and figure out where they and the other participants were. Settling into the display took a few moments at least, in addition to the time it took to switch gear from one participant to another. And, as if those problems were not enough to deal with, the effectors themselves were somewhat fragile—being handled by so many people, they eventually could break down electronically or break apart physically.

Even with just one or two people, the experience of immersive computing could be cumbersome. Effectors generally shut off the outside world to create a sense of immersion in the computer's domain. As long as the participants had enough physical space to move around in, they were fine, but it still felt odd to know they really were in a different area than the one they could see. Finally, there were those who simply disliked the idea of having to wear VR equipment in the first place. These people thought that using gloves, helmets, wands, and other "toys" actually was a worse method of computer interaction than using keyboards, mice, and monitors.

Not surprisingly, a number of people began to think of creating digital spaces the way Myron Krueger had, with interactive computer environments projected onto large display screens. (Krueger himself continued developing various artificial-reality displays throughout the 1980s and 1990s.) Others took a different approach, creating systems that seemed to project computer graphics into the real world, much as the Sword of Damocles display had done. In the process, they created a number of alternative ways to bring people closer to their computers.

Computing in a CAVE

For many researchers, solving the problems of working in virtual environments meant taking the display screens off the human body and making them bigger. In the 1965 paper he wrote about his idea for "The Ultimate Display," Ivan Sutherland stated that the ideal human-computer interface would be a room in which people could order a computer to change the molecular structure of material objects. These days, there are machines that can assemble three-dimensional models of computer-designed objects in a short time, using liquid resins or other substances. The imaginary interface room Sutherland described, though, seems as unlikely to be built in the near future as it seemed in the middle of the 1960s. But in 1991, a group of researchers at the University of Illinois at Chicago developed a room in which computers did the next best thing.

The researchers called their creation the Cave Automatic Virtual Environment, or CAVE for short. The computerized "cave" actually was a cube-shaped room within a room that measured 10 feet on a side. Its walls were rear-projection displays, like a movie theater with projectors behind, rather than in front of, the screens. An overhead projector could, if the researchers desired, beam images onto the CAVE's

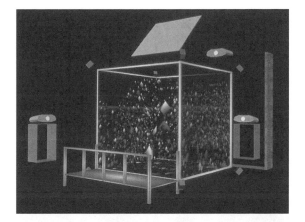

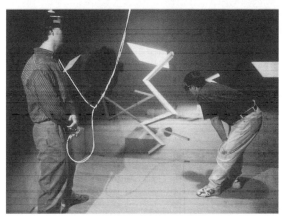

The Cave Automatic Virtual Environment, or CAVE, is one of a number of systems that offer an alternative to HMD-and-glove-style virtual reality. These systems can all trace their conceptual roots back to the work of artificial-reality pioneer Myron Krueger. [©1995 Alan Millman and Sumit Das, Electronic Visualization Laboratory, University of Illinois at Chicago; ©1995 courtesy of Roberta Dupuis-Devlin, Office of Publication Services, University of Illinois at Chicago]

floor to create an even larger environment. The CAVE used shutter glasses to create the illusion of stereo vision, while a set of small speakers handled directional sound effects. CAVE participants manipulated objects and moved around the environment using control wands that were wired into the computers generating the display.

The researchers who designed the CAVE soon discovered that, as they had hoped, this type of projected virtual-reality system was an excellent way to help groups of people work together. People literally could step into or out of a display and know immediately where they and the other participants were in the virtual world. Interacting with the environment could be as simple as moving closer to a screen that showed a particularly interesting detail or a design problem the group was having trouble working out. It also was easier to draw the group's attention to a particular area of the display: All someone had to do was point to it and say, "Look at that."

CAVEs also reduced some of the burden placed on reality engines and other VR components as well. The computers that controlled the display did not have to render separate views for each participant in the CAVE, because everyone saw the same portions of the environment at the same time. The computers also did not have as many position sensors to track: only one tracker for each control wand, one or two for hand motion, and one for each pair of shutter glasses. Nor were people restricted to using just these controllers. In one of the first applications of CAVE to a real-life task, a construction equipment company tested a vehicle design by combining a physical model of the operator's control cab with a CAVE display of the vehicle's body and a simulated construction site. By using the cab controls, a driver could test how the loader might perform.

In the decade since the Chicago researchers put their first CAVE into action, CAVEs have been used for quite a few collaborative virtual-environment projects. At various times, groups of car designers, engineers, architects, molecular researchers, and archaeologists have found CAVEs to be ideal tools for working on complicated or detailed projects. The room-size displays also have served as showcases for video art.

A CAVE display can take up an entire room, or it can be a series of movie screens attached to metal frameworks that people can set up anywhere they find the space. Most CAVEs have fewer display screens—for example, leaving out the ceiling and rear wall—to make setting up and using the system a bit easier. The big drawback to a CAVE display, though, is its cost—up to $1.5 million, depending on how the system is set up. CAVEs use expensive, high-powered workstations to create and display virtual environments, and most CAVE systems are set up at large university research centers, where the costs are shared by companies or government agencies that use them.

Desktop Displays

The same team that created the CAVE realized their techniques could be adapted to a smaller, and more affordable, projected virtual-environment display. A simplified version of the CAVE, the ImmersaDesk, reproduced the CAVE effect with just one screen. In many ways, it was similar to the computer-assisted drafting table that Douglas Engelbart imagined architects using to design buildings. Like the CAVE, the ImmersaDesk displayed images on a rear-projection screen that could be suspended vertically or set at an angle to the users, who either stood or sat in front of the desk. Again, shutter glasses helped create the illusion of depth in the display, while wands and other effectors allowed interaction with the displayed data.

Just as with the CAVE, people had an easier time working together on projects using the desk display than they did using more restrictive methods, or even using standard two-dimensional computer monitors. Even though the display presented a more limited field of view to its users—turning their heads too far in any direction brought them out of the environment—it provided a sufficient sense of depth and immersion. Better still, the desktop displays were both less expensive and easier to install in smaller spaces, making them more attractive to potential customers.

Once the ImmersaDesk and the CAVE were ready for real-world use, the Electronic Visualization Laboratory—the group within the University of Illinois at Chicago that developed the displays—allowed a commercial manufacturer to build and sell the systems in return for a licensing fee. Modern-day ImmersaDesks, like modern-day CAVE systems, are built by Fakespace Systems of Ontario, Canada, one of the oldest immersive-environment equipment manufacturers. However, other companies have developed their own desk-based immersive displays and have helped expand the ways in which these systems can be used.

In general, VR desk displays can be used for the same types of immersive collaboration tasks as CAVE systems. They seem to be especially well suited for scientific research and visualization tasks, such as geology and oil exploration analysis. Because they offer a more personal level of interaction, though, desk displays also are promoted as potentially useful training tools. And many people might indeed benefit from using these displays: factory workers who need to know how to operate new equipment; military personnel who need simulated-mission training to develop basic battle awareness; even emergency service workers such as firemen and police officers who need ongoing preparation in safe high-speed driving techniques.

Some particularly futuristic-looking versions of the virtual-environment desk display use curved rather than flat screens to display digital worlds. Curving the screen of a desk display has two effects. First, it helps shut off the view of everything surrounding the screen, giving the user a chance to focus on his or her work. Second, it rein-

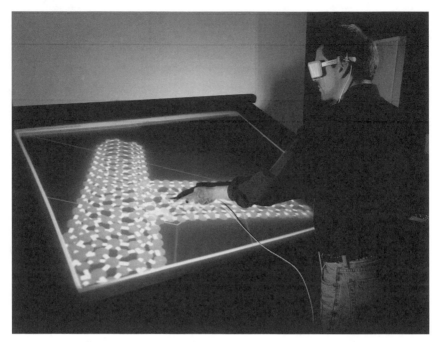

A NASA researcher uses a virtual workbench to demonstrate a molecular modeling experiment. [Courtesy NASA [AMES Research Center]]

forces the illusion of depth not only in a three-dimensional display where shutter glasses come into use but even in strictly two-dimensional projections. People are used to seeing pictures displayed on flat surfaces with straight edges at their boundaries, whether they are computer monitors, movie screens, or even pictures hanging on a wall. Curving the surface of the screen alters the way the eyes perceive images upon it, tricking them into registering a dimension of depth that is not there.

Artificial Reality

Another type of projected VR follows the lead Myron Krueger set with VIDEOPLACE and other artificial-reality environments. Instead of presenting digital environments that wrap around their users, or creating computer-generated figures that people control with wands or gloves, these systems track their users directly with video cameras and incorporate their images and actions into the on-screen world. This way, participants in these environments seem to interact directly with the display, rather than through a go-between device like a wired glove or a wand. Alternate versions of this type of artificial reality include displays that substitute computer-graphic characters for the realistic images of participants.

Krueger himself continued working on projected graphics displays throughout the 1980s and 1990s. One of his projects used an overhead projector to display documents and other objects on a flat-topped desk and a video monitor to keep track of a user's hands. People could handle documents and other objects simply by touching their images and moving them. Another mid-1990s version of this up-to-date artificial reality was developed at MIT's Media Lab. Called ALIVE, or Artificial Life Interactive Video Environment, it combined video images of the user and his or her surroundings with computer graphics to create a system that responds to a participant's actions. One application of ALIVE, called Smart Room, featured a cartoonlike computer-graphics dog that could do various tasks and obey commands, including the command to shake hands with the participant.

Similar systems have appeared at different times around the world. At the California Science Center in Los Angeles, California, visitors can take part in an artificial-reality experience. Watching this exhibit in use is almost as interesting as using it. Visitors stand a few feet away from a large video monitor and select a game from an on-screen menu. In one game, players become soccer goalies defending their net from an onslaught of soccer balls. Once the game starts, the players move back and forth, wave their arms or legs, and duck their heads around to control their on-screen images.

There are still other types of projected or large-scale virtual-environment displays. For immersive, three-dimensional presentations to very large groups of people, a number of companies make display systems that use screens measuring from four feet to more than 20 feet wide. These systems come in handy whenever people need to take in a lot of detail at one time: conducting virtual walk-throughs of airplane designs, giving presentations on architectural projects, even showing people how well a virtual-environment software package can create on-screen images. The main drawback to these projected VR systems is the amount of space they take up. Naturally, one could not stash a CAVE system, for example, in a corner of the family room. At the same time, these systems offer a type of effortless group interaction that is harder to achieve with HMD-and-glove systems.

Augmented Reality

No matter how well a virtual-reality system renders and helps people manage information, there is one level of inconvenience that cannot be overcome. As with many other types of computers, virtual-reality computers are not exactly portable. For most applications, there is little need to work with virtual environments away from the network of computers, displays, and effectors that contain them. Likewise, most standard computer programs are useful only for work that people do while they are sitting at their computers. Some tasks, however, would be faster or easier to accomplish if a computerized database of instructions or other information were nearby, especially if the data could be viewed without having to turn away and look at a small, flat monitor screen. In situations like these, *augmented reality* could come in handy.

Augmented reality is a related technology to virtual reality that uses tools that are the same as or similar to the effectors of VR. The difference between augmented reality, or AR, and VR is the type of data immersion each technology provides. Rather than replacing one's view of the physical world with a data display, AR uses the data to enhance the appearance of real life. A typical augmented reality system features a system of prisms and lenses that reflect computer-generated images into the user's eye. As a result, the images appear to overlay real objects in front of the user.

As with other virtual-environment technologies, there are a number of different ways to display the computer graphics needed to augment the real world. One method being explored is similar to the Sword of Damocles, with prisms and lenses in front of each eye that act as portable heads-up displays. As a result, the device can project three-dimensional graphics that merge with the three-dimensional world. Such a display could be useful for architects, urban planners, and people in similar professions, who could use these displays to see how new buildings would fit in with a neighborhood or where new parks could be placed.

Another type of display uses a single projector-and-prism setup to beam images into the eye. Called a *virtual retinal display*, it is the creation of Dr. Tom Furness and other researchers at the Human Interface Technology Laboratory at the University of Washington, of which Furness is the director. Working prototypes of the display use rapid-moving, low-power laser beams to draw data directly on the retina, creating very sharp images that stand out clearly against the real world.

AR has the potential to become a real benefit to physicians, engineers, and other professionals who do intricate or complex tasks. Using an AR system, an airplane mechanic could project an instruction manual over his or her view of an airplane's engine, with arrows linking portions of diagrams to their real-world counterparts. Physicians could display *X-ray* or *ultrasound* images on their patients as they examined or operated on them.

These applications are a few years away, though. Augmented reality displays still are an experimental technology, and they still need to be developed to the point where they can reliably perform in the real world. A number of hurdles still must be overcome, the biggest of which is developing a way to make computers lay images precisely over real-world objects. Achieving this level of performance is as tricky as getting a virtual environment to function correctly. Even a slight difference between the edge of a solid object and the edge of its projected counterpart is enough for people to notice. Such an error might not be bad if the AR display was designed as a travel guide that labeled historic buildings in a city—tourists eventually would be able to figure out which building was which. However, if the display was designed to show assembly-line workers where to attach a piece of equipment, a slight error might be enough to ruin the machine they were making.

VR AS A
RESEARCH TOOL

Science is not a haphazard process, but one that follows a straight-forward path of investigation. The scientific method of examining and explaining the workings of the physical world takes place in stages: observing a phenomenon; suggesting a hypothesis, or an explanation of what causes the phenomenon; conducting experiments to test the hypothesis; and seeing if the results of the experiments prove or disprove the hypothesis. Finally, for a hypothesis to be considered a valid theory, other scientists have to be able to conduct the same experiments and get the same results.

Virtual-reality systems can help, and in fact have helped, scientists evaluate data and test their theories ever since the technology first became available. One of the first applications of the VIEW system at the NASA Ames Research Center was a project called the Virtual Windtunnel, which was an immersive display for testing the flight characteristics of airplane and shuttle designs. Real wind tunnels are like long, smooth-walled corridors with a large fan at one end. The fan's speed, and in some setups the angle of its blades, can be adjusted to create winds from light breezes to full-blown gales. These structures show how air flows over and presses on model and full-size prototype vehicles. Depending on the size of the model placed inside the wind

NASA's Virtual Windtunnel was an early application of VR technology to engineering. It combined a BOOM display and a wired-glove controller with a high-performance graphics workstation to create digital environments for analyzing aircraft and spacecraft performance. Here, an engineer analyzes how air flows over the surface of a space-shuttle design. [Courtesy NASA [Ames Research Center]]

tunnel, engineers can simulate anything from the stresses on a commercial jet flying at 20,000 feet to the air resistance a car meets traveling at 30 miles per hour.

For all their versatility, though, wind tunnels are expensive to build and run, and setting up experiments can take a lot of time. The Virtual Windtunnel seemed to offer a faster, less expensive way of doing things. In the Virtual Windtunnel, researchers created wireframe models of an airplane or a shuttle and, using a wired glove and a stereoscopic viewer called a BOOM (for Binocular Omni-Orientation Monitor), analyzed how well a vehicle slipped through the atmosphere. The system calculated and rendered the image of air flowing over the model, showing whether the craft traveled smoothly or caused unnecessary turbulence that could interfere with maneuvering or even cause damage. Using the glove, researchers could change variables such as the speed and the angle at which the vehicle moved through the air and focus on different areas of the craft.

As with many of the first applications of virtual reality, the Virtual Windtunnel proved itself a good idea but never went much beyond being a prototype; eventually, it was abandoned. However, as more scientists heard of and gained access to the technology of VR, they began adapting it to their own fields of study. Soon, researchers were applying immersive-computing techniques to such diverse subjects as chemistry, astrophysics, geology, marine biology, and theoretical mathematics (which often uses computer graphics to visualize equations that have complex solutions).

Blowing in the (Virtual) Wind

Meteorology, the study of weather and the atmosphere, is a field that seems tailor-made for virtual-reality applications. Weather is an incredibly complex phenomenon: It combines the effects of air pressure, air temperature, ground temperature, terrain, and a host of other variables. It also is a perfect example of a three-dimensional phenomenon that is difficult to analyze even in a laboratory. Much of what happens in the atmosphere—wind, the process of cloud formation, the interaction of hot and cold fronts—is not visible to the naked eye. All people can see are the results of these interactions, such as clouds forming along the boundaries of two weather systems. And, as with many other sciences, it is not always possible, convenient—or safe—for meteorologists to go out and observe the natural phenomena they want to analyze and explain.

In the mid-1990s, researchers at the Argonne National Laboratory in Illinois (a federally funded research lab that develops and explores the possibilities of cutting-edge technology) used a CAVE to find out how well the system could simulate weather patterns that developed over an area of the United States. As it turned out, the system worked pretty well. The simulation included a three-dimensional terrain map and adjustable controls for air pressure, temperature, and other effects. Long arrows showed which way any wind generated in the simulation would blow, with the color of each arrow indicating whether it was a fresh breeze or a gale. Also, because the winds were computer-graphics models, they could be stopped and reversed while being analyzed.

Wind does not blow as a solid mass of air; instead, many wind streams blow in different directions at different levels in the atmosphere. If these streams were seen from above, they would seem to crisscross each other like reeds in a woven mat. The Argonne simulation reproduced this effect, showing wind patterns at various layers in the atmosphere and revealing points at which winds accelerated or decelerated. Researchers studying these virtual-weather displays used a control wand to travel around the simulation, focusing on high-wind areas or pulling back to get the big picture. They even could track the wind as it blew over the virtual terrain by dropping a computer-generated ribbon that sailed through the simulation.

Other researchers have experimented with more advanced methods of simulating and analyzing weather systems. For a long time, scientists at the National Center for Atmospheric Research (NCAR) in Boulder, Colorado, have used animated computer graphics to analyze data collected on such phenomena as global temperature changes, cloud formation, and the development of severe storm systems. Producing these short computer movies has been an efficient method of showing how these systems form in the atmosphere over time and have allowed scientists to stop and reverse the course of a storm system for detailed analysis (something, of course, that is impossible to do in real life). However, examining the data from more than one angle or isolating just a few elements of the weather system being studied meant generating brand-new animation clips.

In recent years, the NCAR scientists have been including immersive computer-graphic displays of weather systems in their work, using large-screen monitors, shutter glasses, and control wands to examine the data from more than one perspective. These immersive analyses proved themselves useful enough for the center to design a new Visualization Laboratory that incorporates a wall-size, high-definition monitor that can display stereographic views to a group of researchers or to a large audience of visitors to the center.

Force-feedback Soccer in the Microscopic World

Chemistry is another field that is ideally suited for virtual-environment displays. The GROPE-II project at the University of North Carolina's Chapel Hill campus, in fact, was an early attempt to create a digital

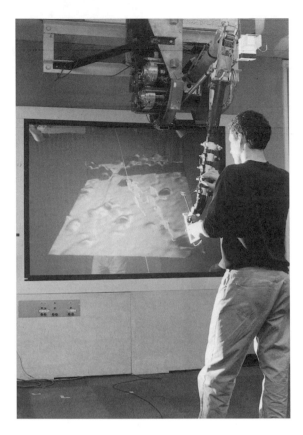

Mike Falvo, a researcher at the University of North Carolina at Chapel Hill, uses the university's modified ARM to work with the nanoManipulator system. Aided by force-feedback cues from the nanoManipulator, UNC researchers can move objects that are measured on the nanometer scale.
[Courtesy University of North Carolina at Chapel Hill, Department of Computer Science]

environment for exploring and experimenting with chemical reactions. Though the computers of the 1970s were not quite up to the challenge of the work Frederick Brooks and his fellow researchers wished to do, the computers of the 1980s and early 1990s were sufficiently advanced to handle a modified version of the project, GROPE-III.

Researchers interacted with the computer display using an Argonne Remote Manipulator (ARM), a large remote-control device for nuclear plant workers. In nuclear plants, the postlike ARM transferred workers' hand and arm movements to robotic arms that handled nuclear materials inside shielded workspaces. For GROPE-II, Frederick Brooks and his colleagues fitted the ARM with a combination of electric motors that turned the manipulator into a force-feedback effector. Before long, researchers were able to juggle computer-generated molecules of up to 1,500 atoms with the ARM while watching a projected 3-D display.

The modified ARM simulated the physical reactions of the molecules by pushing or pulling the user's hand and arm. Real molecules carry slight charges that attract molecules to one another or push them apart, depending on the molecules' chemical makeup. If the GROPE-II operator tried to link two virtual molecules that repelled each other, the ARM would suddenly stop moving. If the virtual molecules were attracted to each other, the ARM would pop forward slightly, indicating a successful docking.

GROPE-II, in its various versions, provided years of good service to the computer scientists and chemists who used it in their experiments. Then UNC researchers began using a different force-feedback device, the PHANTOM haptic manipulator developed by Thomas Massie at MIT and later sold by a company he helped found called SensAble Technologies. Working in virtual environments with the desktop-mounted PHANTOM and its single-finger interface was easier than handling the extra mass of the larger, bulkier ARM. (For one

In another version of UNC's nanoManipulator, Mike Falvo uses a PHANTOM force-feedback device to work with microscopic objects. The shutter glasses he is wearing turn the image on the computer monitor into a three-dimensional display.
[Courtesy University of North Carolina at Chapel Hill, Department of Computer Science]

thing, researchers could sit down while using the PHANTOM.) PHANTOM gradually replaced the ARM as the main effector in a number of projects, primarily in UNC's experimental nanoManipulator program, which offered scientists the opportunity to work directly in the realm of the very small. NanoManipulator was an example of how people can use VR to control machines in remote, dangerous, or inaccessible locations. This kind of remote control through virtual reality is called telerobotics, teleoperation, or telepresence.

Researchers used the system to work with objects measured in nanometers, distances of one billionth of a meter (.000000039 inch). Objects this small are made visible by using scanning probe microscopes. A scanning probe microscope scans an extremely tiny needle-like probe back and forth over objects placed in the microscope's testing chamber. One type of probe uses a beam of electrons to keep a fixed distance above these objects; another type triggers a motor in the microscope that raises the probe when it touches an obstruction in its path. The microscope creates a video image of the objects the probe travels over based on how high it has to lift the probe. By carefully handling the probe, researchers can move objects with the probe's tip or with the electron beam the probe emits.

The nanoManipulator displayed the microscope's data in a 3-D virtual environment rendered on a desktop computer monitor. Shutter glasses turned the monitor's flat display into a stereoscopic simulation. Using the nanoManipulator, UNC researchers studied how well electricity flows through viruses by moving them into tiny electric circuits. The ability of a virus to conduct electricity, its electric potential, can tell scientists much about the virus's physical and chemical makeup. UNC scientists even nudged tiny particles of gold through gaps in equally tiny gold wires like athletes kicking soccer balls though solid gold goals.

Researchers with the National Aeronautics and Space Administration also developed a system that gave people the ability to feel and move atoms, though these were merely virtual-reality models. The system was a model of *mechanosynthesis*, the ability to assemble extremely tiny mechanisms atom by atom, with each atom lining up in a specific position. A researcher worked at an Immersive Workbench (made by Fakespace Systems), donned a pair of stereographic shutter glasses, and picked up a small control wand to move computer-graphic atoms either in groups or separately.

The goal of this "Virtual Mechanosynthesis," or VMS, display was to show how researchers in the growing field of nanotechnology could

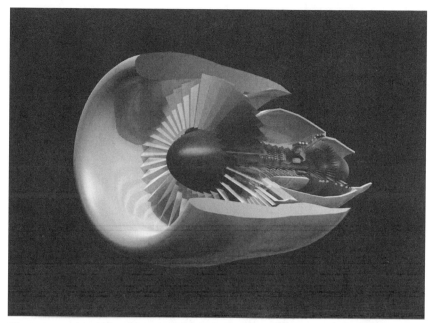

Three-dimensional computer graphics techniques used in computer aided design systems also can be applied to scientific and engineering simulations in VR.
(Image courtesy: VR Sim, Inc.)

create and program the miniscule assemblers that actually would create machines from individual atoms. To make the simulation more realistic, the VMS also could incorporate a haptic controller that simulated the forces attracting and repelling each atom in the display. As with GROPE-II, when an atom was placed correctly, the controller would tug slightly as the atom nestled into position. When the user tried to force the atom into a position it would not go to in the real world, they would feel it being pushed aside.

Running Experiments in Virtual Labs

Just as virtual-reality displays can provide control over miniscule objects, they can simulate larger environments to which a researcher might need access. A few years ago, a team of researchers at UIC and at Wayne State University in Detroit, Michigan, used the CAVE to build a virtual environment called SANDBOX in which scientists could simulate their data or data from other scientists' work. (SAND-BOX was short for "Scientists Accessing Necessary Data Based On eXperimentation.") In the SANDBOX, a scientist could verify the results of an experiment by re-creating it using graphic representations of lab equipment. Conceivably, any experiment could have been reenacted, as long as its procedure and results were available in easily accessed computer files, or databases. The SANDBOX also was designed to allow the scientist to browse through related databases to retrieve information or to conduct a rapid search for a specific bit of knowledge.

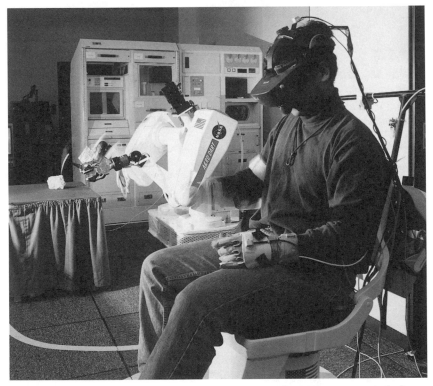

Virtual-reality tools have been used for experiments in long-distance control of machinery as well as for interaction in digital environments. Here, researcher Larry Li, a project engineer for the Dextrous Anthropomorphic Robotic Testbed, demonstrates how a VR-controlled robot could gather rock samples on distant planets. [Courtesy of NASA]

The CAVE display system has been used for many scientific and mathematical simulations. This image shows a Julia Set, a map of how a complex equation behaves when its results are fed back into itself. Displaying the results of equations such as these in a stereoscopic, three-dimensional form can give mathematicians an added level of insight into higher mathematics. [© 1995 Daniel J. Sandin and Joe Insley, Electronic Visualization Laboratory, and Louis H. Kauffman and Yumei Dang, Department of Mathematics, Statistics and Computer Science, University of Illinois at Chicago]

While the virtual experiment was running, the scientist could display other related data. He or she could review notes written by other researchers, examine maps or photographs taken of real-world locations related to the experiment, even hang graphs of previous experiments on surrounding virtual walls. The scientist also could use more than just the sense of sight to interpret data. SANDBOX's designers incorporated sound effects into the environment, such as the sound of fluids dripping into beakers in a chemistry lab. SANDBOX's creators even used unusual sounds to represent some measurements, such as playing the high-pitched buzz of a cicada to represent the average temperature of a series of thermometers. The cicada buzz increased as the temperature rose and grew silent as things cooled down.

The quest to develop virtual environments for scientific collaboration tools has continued, though it has taken on other forms. One form is the Chesapeake Bay Virtual Environment, a project under development in Norfolk, Virginia, at Old Dominion University's Virtual Environments Laboratory. Using CAVE and ImmersaDesk displays, scientists in the university's Center for Coastal Physical Oceanography are working on a realistic model of the world beneath the waves in and around the Chesapeake Bay. Researchers at Old Dominion constantly monitor the bay's tides, temperatures, winds, and other environmental data using sensors placed on land and under water. With this information, the scientists are developing a series of simulations of the bay ecosystem, including views of how tide and wave action distribute foreign particles.

Another type of scientific visualization environment has a more economically oriented purpose. Exploring for oil can be a difficult, time-consuming process; petroleum geologists can spend months in the field surveying sites where oil might be found and months more analyzing the data they collect to identify the most promising places to drill. Part of this work includes the seismic analysis of a potential oil field, setting off explosives to send shock waves deep into the ground and recording the waves that are reflected back to the surface. Just as analyzing the delay in how radar beams bounce back from objects can reveal the difference between a cloud bank and an airplane, analyzing these artificial earthquake waves will reveal fault lines, mineral deposits, and other features within the ground.

This is a lot of information to have to search through. A few geologic exploration companies, however, are using immersive-display systems to speed up the process, allowing geologists to "fly" through data that has been color coded to reveal subsurface details. The Phillips Petroleum Company developed one such display late in the 1990s. It uses a color projector to beam data onto a nearly 36-foot-square display screen with an arch-shaped, semicircular dome in its center. This dome provides a sense of depth even without the use of shutter glasses or other stereographic effectors. If a geologist wants to get a look at a three-dimensional section within the larger display, he or she can use a smaller handheld screen that is monitored with a magnetic position tracker. As the researcher moves the smaller screen about, the projector displays a separate window of information that covers the screen's surface.

Another oil and gas exploration firm, the Murphy Oil Company Ltd., of Calgary, Canada, began using a different method to analyze seismic data in 2001. Instead of building its own system, as Phillips Petroleum had done, the company bought a wall-style virtual-environment display made by Silicon Graphics Inc. and Fakespace Systems.

The company was exploring for oil off the eastern coast of Canada and needed a faster way to identify likely drilling spots that were deep under water. The company decided to turn the seismic data into an immersive environment so its scientists and engineers could work together at the same time and be able to identify and analyze small details within the large mass of data they had to handle.

Re-forming Dinosaurs Through Scientific Visualization

Three-dimensional computer graphics do not have to be immersive to have real-world scientific benefits. Ever since 1905, a mounted fossil skeleton of the three-horned, plant-eating dinosaur *Triceratops* has been one of the best-known dinosaurs at the National Museum of Natural History in Washington, D.C. When scientists assembled the display back then, however, they did not know as much about dinosaurs as modern paleontologists do today. Also, they did not have a complete *Triceratops* skeleton to work with. As a result, they assembled the display with a good dose of guesswork, combining parts of different *Triceratops* fossils and handcrafting missing pieces to create what they thought would be a good representation of the animal. (They even used bits of an entirely different dinosaur to form the rear feet of the displayed skeleton, as no one had discovered those parts of a *Triceratops* in 1905.)

By the late 1990s, the fossilized bones were beginning to deteriorate. To preserve them for future study, the museum decided to repair the skeleton and replace many of the less stable bones with plaster casts. At the same time, the museum corrected the errors that had been put in more than 90 years before. As part of this work, a team of scientists and technicians scanned the bones (the real *Triceratops* bones, that is) with a low-power laser and used this information to create a digitized version of the exhibit. With all the bones present in the computer, scientists were able to create better quality replacements for the missing or incorrectly placed pieces. All they had to do was create the mirror image of a bone on the opposite side of the dinosaur's body or scan in a cast of the correct bone from a similar-size *Triceratops* that they obtained from another museum.

The digitized bones also gave the scientists the opportunity to figure out how the dinosaur moved and walked. In the past, people thought that dinosaurs were slow-moving, somewhat clumsy creatures, and they displayed dinosaur fossils in positions that reinforced this belief. These days, paleontologists have a better idea of how dinosaurs' bones and muscles fit together, thanks, in part, to three-dimensional computer modeling tools. The scientists studying the natural history museum's *Triceratops* used the digitized bone images to create small-scale plastic replicas of the fossils, which fit together in what they believed was the best possible configuration. This, as one scientist said, was something that could not be done using the multiton original fossils.

Another thing that could not be done with the fossils was get them to move; however, using the three-dimensional computer version and an animation program, the museum researchers were able to work out how *Triceratops* might have walked when it was alive. Using the plastic model and the computer graphics, scientists were able to show that the dinosaur stood with its legs more or less straight under its body and that it could possibly have run as fast as a rhinoceros, up to 30 miles an hour.

VR AS A
TRAINING TOOL

Virtual reality can show people worlds they might not see any other way, and they can give people the ability to do things they could not do anyplace else. On the other hand, virtual reality also gives people the ability to see and do things they *can* do elsewhere, but in a safe, controlled setting. This makes VR an ideal training tool for people who have dangerous or simply complicated jobs.

In virtual environments, soldiers and sailors can build or hone the skills they need to survive during combat. New employees can learn how to get around in unfamiliar and hazardous conditions without risking an on-site accident. Experienced workers can refresh their skills in realistically reproduced working conditions. And companies can examine their facilities for ways to make conditions safer, even to the point of looking over factory floors before they are built.

At least, this way of thinking has been behind the idea of training people in immersive environments. As with other aspects of virtual reality, though, not too many systems have been created specifically for worker training. A number of studies showed that people benefit from exposure to simulated workplaces, but these systems cost so much that few industries could afford them. Even so, just as scientists keep finding new ways to apply VR to their research, government and big business researchers keep finding ways to train people in digitized worlds.

Virtual Reality in the Military

When most people use VR to simulate hazardous environments or difficult tasks, they are looking for ways to minimize their risks. When members of the armed forces use VR to simulate hazardous environments or difficult tasks, they are simply preparing for a day at the office. For members of the armed forces, "the office" can be a block of sky that opposing air forces wish to control, a battlefield, or a stretch of harbor leading to the open ocean. All of these locales, and many others, are being simulated in virtual reality.

Things happen so quickly in combat that soldiers, sailors, and pilots can easily become overwhelmed. Armies, navies, and air forces train constantly to keep this from happening, preparing for the time their skills are called upon. Since the fall of the Soviet Union in the early

Modern flight simulators come in many shapes and sizes. The three-screen display, cockpit mock-up, and controlling computer can be disassembled and sent to various air bases far more easily than can larger, full-motion simulators. [Evans & Sutherland Computer Corp.]

Airplane and helicopter flight simulators are some of the most widely used virtual-reality training systems. (Evans & Sutherland Computer Corp.)

1990s, however, nations around the world have been shrinking their armed forces and spending less money on the troops who are left. Budget cuts mean that armed forces cannot do as much real-life training as they might need. Combat exercises risk the lives of the people who are involved, cost millions of dollars, and put an enormous amount of wear and tear on equipment. With less money available, many services around the world are developing ways to mimic military tasks in the relatively cheaper arena of VR.

Remember, the first truly immersive interactive environment and the technology that displayed it were created for fighter pilots. Unfortunately, the SuperCockpit program, which could have become a high-tech tool for controlling warplanes, was abandoned in the late 1980s, when the U.S. Air Force decided that creating virtual-environment substitutes for or enhancements of physical flight controls would be too expensive. Even using the head-mounted display for flight simulation was stretching the technology that had been developed for the demonstration model of SuperCockpit. With the boom in computer technology of the 1980s and 1990s, though, the quality of military (and civilian) flight simulators skyrocketed.

Fighter pilots can train in full-scale cockpits placed inside minitheaters mounted on motion platforms; dome-shaped screens surround the pilots with simulated scenes of airports and cloud-filled skies. As the pilot "flies" the simulator, the motion platform tilts and shakes to provide the sensations of flight. Other systems use nonmoving cockpits with smaller, flat-screen displays that still give much of the feeling of air-to-air combat.

Improvements in computer graphics alone have contributed much to the quality of the simulation. Instead of grid-shaped landscapes and simplified icons of hostile targets, such as those in VCASS, modern simulators allow pilots to fly over realistic terrain and engage true-to-life enemy aircraft. Some simulators monitor which way their pilots look, using motion trackers attached to standard helmets, and adjust the display accordingly.

A Wide Distribution of Military VR

Fixed-wing aircraft are not the only military vehicles that are being simulated in VR. In the United States alone, a host of virtual war machines, from the AH-64A Apache helicopter to the M1A1 Abrams tank, have computerized counterparts that combine physical mock-ups with immersive computer displays. As an added benefit, simulators in separate cities, separate states, and even separate countries will eventually be linked for large-scale simulated combat missions. A system called Distributed Interactive Simulation, DIS, is being developed to link many different types of simulators to a shared virtual battlefield. Such a widely distributed system would help the various services avoid a serious problem that crops up during wartime: the difficulty in synchronizing the actions of the thousands of troops, vehicles, and weapons during wartime. No major battle is ever unplanned. Aside from chance meetings between small fighting units, in every engagement both sides start out following carefully drawn plans. Each service receives orders describing where troops will move, where artillery and aircraft will bombard enemy positions, or where warships will launch rockets, land troops, or engage enemy shipping. These plans rarely last beyond the first few minutes of a battle, but they always are available at the start.

Part of the reason why battle plans almost never last is that the thousands of soldiers, vehicles, and weapons involved have usually

Virtual-training environments can simulate any conditions a trainee might face in the real world. This scene shows how a military staging area might look in daylight. (Image courtesy: www.5dt.com)

never worked together on a grand scale. Invariably, things will go wrong. A tank group will move out at the wrong time or will lose track of where it is; a communications relay will break down; a squadron of ground attack planes will be prevented from supporting allied troops by heavy antiaircraft fire. The commanding officers of all the forces involved have to work around such problems in a matter of minutes, if not seconds, to keep the tide of battle from turning against them. Such rapid adjustments can cause further problems or they can succeed, depending on how well the forces involved work together. DIS training, by combining simulators from various branches of the military, can help build these needed techniques of teamwork.

Individual soldiers also would benefit from learning to handle the stresses of combat in virtual environments. Unlike war movies, real combat is not choreographed. Every instant spent advancing through a combat zone or patrolling unfamiliar territory exposes soldiers to a spectrum of real and possible dangers. Enemy snipers can suddenly open fire from inside a building. Booby-trapped explosives can wipe out whole squads in an instant. Even normally harmless things, like fog, can hide potential dangers to an advancing unit. Training mentally prepares men and women to handle these dangers as much as it exposes them to the techniques of fighting. Researchers at such institutions as the Naval Postgraduate School in Monterey, California, and STRI-COM—the U.S. Army's Simulation, Training, and Instrumentation Command—in Orlando, Florida, have been working on VR systems that can help give soldiers the edge in battle.

The Dismounted Infantry Virtual Environment (DIVE) program was one such system. It combined virtual environments developed for use with DIS simulators with single-person VR effectors, including special wired replicas of the weapons normally carried into combat. It also used highly realistic computer-generated soldiers as participants in the simulated missions. With such a system, a trainee squad leader (an experienced soldier who is in charge of a group of up to 10 others) could issue orders to a squad of virtual troops as if they were in a real firefight. Such virtual missions might include clearing out a building full of enemy troops that also are created by the computer.

Even simple levels of computer simulation have been explored to see if they can offer useful training. In mid-1990s, the United States Marine Corps's Systems Command division experimented with a modified version of the computer combat game DOOM to train marines in the techniques of urban combat. The add-in package transformed DOOM's three-dimensional landscapes into a computerized replica of a small city street, and the game's monsters into well-armed human foes (as represented by images of toy soldiers). The trainer was not designed as an immersive environment, but one that could be used on inexpensive, easily transported personal computers that could be set up almost anywhere. Another system that the marines have considered using places a computer-generated image in the targeting sight of a life-size, shoulder-mounted missile launcher. Rather than going to the risk and expense of firing live missiles for targeting practice, troops can use the missile trainer to scan for virtual enemy vehicles, launch a simulated missile, and learn if their shot was on target.

To the Sea in Simulated Ships

Military simulators can be used to simulate a host of noncombat environments as well. One such environment being tested out by the United States Navy trains submarine officers how to navigate surfaced subs through harbors. Surface navigation is a very tricky operation. Not only do submarines weigh thousands of tons and cost millions of dollars, but the officer in charge of safely steering through a harbor could effectively end his career if he runs the sub aground or hits another vessel. A young officer has very little time, though, to learn to be an officer of the deck (the official term for this position). Submarines spend most of their time submerged and very little time sailing through harbors.

The simulator, developed by the Naval Research Laboratory's Advanced Technology Branch, is called the Virtual Environment for Submarine Ship Handling Training, or VESUB for short. It uses a head-mounted display and a physical replica of the top portion of a submarine's conning tower to immerse the trainees in the virtual display.

Another vital noncombat task that requires a lot of training is fighting fires on board ship. A fire is one of the most serious disasters that can befall a ship. Many sailors prefer the idea of having a hole punched into the hull of their ship to having a fire break out. A hole can be patched fairly quickly; sailors are trained to use mattresses, lockers, spare wood, and anything else handy as temporary plugs. Even if the hole cannot be patched, naval vessels are equipped with watertight doors that can isolate any flooding to a few compartments.

But a fire on board a ship can quickly get out of hand; almost every space in a ship contains fuel, oil, ammunition, paint, or other flammables that fires can feed on. And when these materials burn, they give off thick smoke and poisonous gases that can rapidly fill the compartments inside the ship's hull. Even with the fire-fighting gear carried aboard every ship, sailors can find themselves on the losing side of a battle with a fire if they are not careful. In the 1990s, the Naval Research Laboratory worked on a VR system to give sailors a greater edge over fires. Their system was based on a virtual replica of the ex-USS *Shadwell*, an old troop landing ship that the navy uses to conduct experiments with new fire-fighting techniques and equipment. The computerized environment can replicate the many types of fires that have broken out in navy ships over the years.

The virtual *Shadwell* proved its potential worth as a training tool in exercises that paired it with the real training vessel. Two teams of experienced navy firefighters were given the task of navigating through the real ship as if they were putting out a fire. To make the task realistic, the faceplates of the firefighters' masks were partially obscured to give the effect of looking through billowing clouds of smoke. The firefighters who explored the virtual environment before going through the physical exercise did better than those who only studied the ship's blueprints. In one case, the crew that went through the VR simulation performed the physical drill roughly half a minute faster. Half a minute may not sound like such a great achievement, but in the real world half a minute can mean the difference between saving and losing a ship and its crew.

Cruising Around Virtual Streets

Safe vehicle operation also is vital in the civilian world, especially for people whose job is to fly, drive, or steer passengers and cargo safely across town or around the world. Simulators that accurately reproduce the conditions these professionals might encounter in their work can prepare them to avoid problems before they occur and safely handle predicaments they cannot escape. These simulators also can evaluate a driver or a pilot's performance, revealing any difficulties in handling situations that can be corrected with extra training.

Commercial flight simulators, which have been in use for decades, are an example of such training and evaluation applications. Airline pilots have benefited from computer simulations as much as fighter pilots. Just as military flight simulators led to the technology of virtual reality, virtual-reality technology has done much to improve the quality of civilian flight simulators. With computer graphics, flight simulators can place pilots at or above almost any major airport in the world. The pilots sit in a realistic mock-up of an airplane cabin and view the computer-generated representation of an airport approach or of a midair flight scene. The experience is made more realistic if the mock-up is placed on a motion platform, a hydraulically controlled tilting table that can change the angle of the simulator. For all practical purposes, however, flight simulators as detailed as these *are* virtual reality: They use computers to generate and control realistic, three-dimensional environments that react to the actions of their participants.

The success airline companies experienced with flight simulator training inspired VR researchers and companies to create similar setups for other applications. One particularly popular area of research involves designing driving simulators that can be used for a host of safety studies and driver training programs. Many of these proposed driving simulators are remarkably similar to flight simulators, but without the type of controls that simulate flight. However, these simulators are able to recreate the sensations of driving through hilly countryside, along rough sections of roadway, or over rain-slick highways.

Air traffic control is one of the most stressful jobs a person can do. Virtual reality has been explored both as a tool for teaching this skill and as a means for making the job easier. [Image courtesy: www.5dt.com]

One of the most ambitious of these simulators is the National Advanced Driving Simulator (NADS), which began operating as the Iowa Driving Simulator at the University of Iowa's Center for Computer-Aided Design in 1992. The NADS is a fully enclosed dome that contains the body of a car or a light truck, complete with its passenger compartment, driver controls, and re-creations of its steering and braking systems. Like a flight simulator, the driving simulator is mounted on a motion platform that mimics the effects of acceleration and road vibration. Using the simulator, researchers study how drivers react to a range of driving conditions, determine if changes in highway design are beneficial, and run virtual prototyping tests of new vehicle designs and machinery. The simulator has even been used for medical research, through monitoring the effects of various medicines on drivers and evaluating the safety of a new type of prescription lens for glasses.

Other driving simulators are available for training military and civilian truck drivers. One of the first civilian VR driving simulators, named "truck driVR," was developed in 1996 for Amoco, the Chicago-based American Oil Company. Every year, all of Amoco's truck drivers are tested by human evaluators who ride with them for a day. Amoco needed a reliable system that could replace this costly, time-consuming way of doing things. The truck driVR mimicked the sensations of driving a tractor-trailer rig filled with 40,000 gallons of gasoline. The oil company hired a firm, which designed computerized training programs, to build a system that combined a steering wheel and foot pedals designed for race-car computer games, an HMD, and a highly detailed virtual environment complete with roads, highways, and other vehicles. The hardware alone cost less than $50,000, an amazing deal considering that such a system would have cost more than $300,000 a year or two earlier. For their money, Amoco got a system that could mimic 21 typical driving hazards (overly aggressive drivers, pedestrians crossing the street at the wrong time, deer jumping in front of the truck) without risking the drivers, their cargo, or any bystanders.

In the half decade since then, truck-driving simulators have become much more sophisticated. Some of these virtual vehicle systems are like the NADS, with a full-size truck cab that sits close to a wraparound display screen. Others use less intricate displays, placing a truck seat and dashboard in front of a large-screen monitor displaying two-dimensional images of city streets and highways. Using these simulators, drivers can learn how to drive defensively, avoid accidents while driving at night or in bad weather, handle various types of roads, and even drive off paved streets. Some simulators even have the ability to feed vibration cues through their steering columns and driver seats, giving trainees a feel for how trucks handle in different situations.

People who have to drive fast in an emergency also are using driving simulators to hone their abilities. Police officers, firefighters, and paramedics in some medium-size and large cities have begun to use mock-ups of their vehicles to practice high-speed chases. These trainers use virtual environments that reproduce the streets and highways the emergency service workers travel in real life. As with the truck-driving simulators, the virtual patrol cars and ambulances can reproduce most of the driving conditions of real life, throwing in hazards such as bad-weather drivers who ignore sirens.

VR-based driver safety training is not limited to four-wheeled vehicles. In Japan, the Kawasaki Motorcycle Company joined with a British VR firm to create a highly realistic motorcycle-driving trainer. Putting on a head-mounted display, a student motorcycle rider mounts a real Kawasaki motorcycle that itself is mounted on a motion platform. As the student navigates the virtual-driving environment, the motorcycle tilts, jitters, and otherwise responds to his or her movements. As with car- and truck-driving simulators, the Kawasaki simulator lets students make and learn from driving mistakes without risking their lives or the lives of other people.

Virtual Industrial Training

VR simulations of hazardous environments could benefit factory workers as much as they help soldiers or truck drivers. One of the most dangerous situations a factory worker faces is the factory floor itself during his or her first weeks on the job. New workers have to spend a lot of time gaining the experience needed to safely work even with a factory's least dangerous machines. New workers also have to spend a great deal

Industrial crane operation, driving, and other tasks have been subjects for VR training. This scene depicts how VR could be used to help train workers to repair and maintain elevators. [Image courtesy: VR Sim, Inc.]

of time getting used to how their factories are arranged. With immersive models of actual workspaces, companies could cut down the time it takes newly hired employees to learn how to do their jobs safely.

However, simulating the conditions of factory work has proven to be a more difficult matter than mimicking other activities. The fact is, virtual-environment training costs too much and until now has been too limited in its effects for most companies to afford to provide such training. For the most part, the only customers for VR-training systems have been very large companies that need to train a lot of workers.

There are a few exceptions to this rule. Manufacturers such as car companies have developed interactive safety training and evaluation systems that safely expose workers to the hazards of life on the factory floor, such as being pinned between a wall and a forklift that is backing up. Using these training systems, workers learn how something as simple as walking over to a drinking fountain can become dangerous if they are not careful.

15

VR AS A TEACHING TOOL

Computers have been educational tools since the days of ENIAC and the vacuum-tube-based computers that followed its construction. Though the engineers and scientists who designed these systems were experts in their fields, the machines served as training tools for a host of students who were seeking master's degrees and doctorates in electrical engineering, physics, mathematics, psychology, and other high-level academic disciplines. Even military computers, such as the interactive SAGE early-warning system, involved the efforts of advanced-level students who learned their subjects as much through hands-on work as through book studies.

These days, of course, computers are present in all levels of the academic world, from elementary schools to universities. Students use computers to learn mathematics and reading, to find information for reports and term papers, to track down books in libraries, and even, in some cases, to send in homework. In the early days of virtual reality, many researchers and teachers thought that the new technology would continue this trend. They believed that students soon would start interacting with virtual environments to learn complicated subjects such as geometry or trigonometry. History lessons might include "field trips" to digitized versions of ancient communities, battlefields, or other historic locations, where the students could see that there was more to the world in times past than the words and the motionless pictures in their textbooks. Chemistry students might gain new levels of insight by conducting experiments with individual molecules, while biology students might see how "living" plants and animals work from the inside, rather than dissecting dead specimens.

As it turned out, virtual reality has had a very small effect on education. The expense of setting up VR systems, the trouble involved in keeping the equipment up and running, and the limited quality of virtual environments that have been developed so far all have kept schools from investing heavily in immersive educational computing. Most educational applications of VR have been special demonstration projects conducted by university researchers or museums. Even so, there have been some applications of educational virtual reality that show its potential for the future, both for use in classrooms and for presenting educational material to people of all ages.

Classroom Virtual Reality

The high cost of virtual-reality systems has not kept educators from trying to bring VR into their classrooms on their own. Even at times when many fully immersive virtual-reality systems cost tens of thousands of dollars, teachers developed their own, less expensive methods for virtually enveloping students in their studies. One of these low-budget projects took place at the Kelly Walsh High School in Casper, Wyoming. In the mid-1990s, computer-programming teacher Becky Underwood developed a way to teach students how to create virtual environments on desktop computers. Her students wore shutter glasses that turned images on the 2-D computer monitors into 3-D displays. They handled virtual objects with modified PowerGloves, control devices based on the VPL Research DataGlove that were manufactured by the Mattel toy company for Nintendo video games. To move around the environments, the students used computer mice or joysticks. And, at the end of each semester, they examined their creations with head-mounted display that cost about $400. Altogether, each of the school's 15 VR systems cost less than $2,500 to put together, with most of that money going to buy the computer that controlled the system.

As simple as the systems were, Underwood's students used them to create some remarkably sophisticated learning environments. One student, who was also studying Latin, used her computer to create a "Latin villa." Each room of the villa linked objects with Latin vocabulary words. As visitors left the villa, they were quizzed on the words they learned. Another student used his knowledge of calculus to create striking three-dimensional models of mathematical equations. One student even reproduced Fort Casper, the 19th-century U.S. Army fort that developed into the city of Casper, as a lesson in local history.

Other teachers showed how younger students could benefit from VR, even if they did not take part in creating virtual environments themselves. The Virtual Reality Roving Vehicle (VRRV), a project of the HIT Lab in Seattle, took a van filled with VR equipment to a number of schools in the Pacific Northwest. The VRRV acted as a supplement to the subjects being studied in each school. In one typical application, the VRRV helped four classes at a junior high school study wetlands (such as swamps and shallow lakes). Working together, the four classes built a VR model of a typical wetland. One class worked on the water cycle, how water enters a marsh or a pond and is used by the plants and animals within it. The other three classes worked on how wetlands collect and use energy, carbon (an element found in all living things), and nitrogen (another element that is especially important to plant life). When completed, the virtual wetland contained simulated plant and animal life, including bacteria that fixed nitrogen in the soil. The students then donned head-mounted displays and explored their virtual environment and compared it to another model that had been created elsewhere.

Projects such as these in the middle of the 1990s closely represented the way educators believed that virtual reality would enter the classroom. Each class, the experts thought, would have access to reality engines and a network of gloves, goggles, and other effectors to take each student into an educational environment. At the very least, there would be a central VR lab that each class in a school would share. However, many of the educators who were considering getting involved in virtual reality, despite its cost, shifted their attention to the astounding rise of a new communications medium, the World Wide Web. Education researchers became more interested in the idea of using the Web to create long-distance learning systems, rather than developing immersive teaching environments. The new vision was for such events as a collaborative Web hookup between two or more classes in different parts of the world that would join forces to complete a large project, thereby learning about one another's cultures as they completed their lessons.

VR on Campus

Despite the drop in projects pairing virtual reality and education, though, the idea of teaching students by using immersive graphical environments still is alive. Past successes with using VR, in fact, have helped spur the development of current projects. At the University of Michigan in Ann Arbor, for example, chemical engineering professors John Bell and H. Scott Fogler developed a series of virtual environments for their Virtual Reality in Chemical Engineering Laboratory (VRiChEL). This gave students the chance to study the operation of chemical reactors and the design of chemical plants virtually firsthand. Classroom lectures and textbook study can only go so far when dealing with highly detailed technical subjects such as these. The only way students truly can understand how these systems work is to see them in action for themselves. Even better, students should be able to fiddle around with a chemical reactor's controls and see how their changes help or hinder reactions.

Bell and Fogler built a set of virtual environments they called VICHER modules—meaning Virtual Chemical Reaction—to give their students a safe way to gain this hands-on experience. Chemical plants are very hazardous operations, and the people in charge of them do not usually open them up to college tour groups. Those plants that do allow student tours restrict them to safe areas away from the main work areas and naturally do not allow students any opportunities for hands-on work. The VICHER modules not only provided simulated versions of real-world equipment but also let students watch simulated chemical reactions taking place inside the simulated reactors. This type of observation, of course, would be impossible in the real world.

In papers they wrote on their work, however, Bell and Fogler pointed out that it will be a while before VICHER and environments like it would be ready to serve as a full-fledged education and research tool. Most of the 155 chemical plant design students who participated in VICHER's first trial run agreed that the simulator was impressive, but most of them also agreed that the system itself needed work. They found that the head-mounted display's graphics were too small and blurry to be of much use. In an article on a different virtual environment—one that provided a tour of a chemical plant's hazards and safety systems—Bell and Fogler mentioned that all the students had to peek under the HMD at a regular computer monitor to read the signs posted in the virtual chemical plant. Still, the students also said that once VR technology improved, these VR applications would be very useful study and research tools.

Bell and Fogler continued collaborating on adapting virtual reality to collegiate studies, though Bell later moved to the University of Illinois at Chicago, where he set up the university's Virtual Reality Undergraduate Projects Laboratory (VRUPL). There, researchers and students have been developing a series of VR simulations of a laboratory to provide a better method of teaching lab safety than giving students or technicians a set of written rules; maintaining and distributing the VRiChEL environments developed at the University of Michigan; and working on a VR map of the university campus for visitors and new students. As part of the lab safety project, VRUPL also has been working on a simulation that gives students the opportunity to design and operate a reactor. If the design is a good one, the students make money; if not, the reactor might blow up. Some of these projects have been developed as VRML files for use on the Web, while others are still being developed for fully immersive systems.

Other three-dimensional learning environments have appeared on the Web. Middle schools in the United States, veterinary colleges in Italy, architecture schools in Spain, science museums in both hemispheres, and other educational institutions have used the same programming techniques of graphics-based on-line communities to create educational worlds. Avatars represent students and teachers who use VRML-style interfaces to take part in interactive lessons that have been incorporated into the landscape. Some of these on-line environments are projects that teams of researchers designed to test their ideas for teaching in virtual environments. Other environments are student projects that give high school and college students the opportunity to study, create, and work within virtual worlds, learning and applying lessons that have real-world applications. In worlds such as these, architecture students can assemble and analyze models of buildings they have designed, while college freshmen can take a three-dimensional tour of their new school before they set foot on campus.

Preserving the Past with VR

Education is not confined to the classrooms of public schools and universities but is something that takes place throughout peoples' lives. Likewise, virtual-reality educational environments can be found wherever a group of people has something interesting to teach others. One of the greatest lessons VR can help teach is how people in past eras lived. History is much more than a timeline of discoveries, wars, plagues, and other events spread out during the growth and decline of nations. At their best, history and the related field of archaeology—the study of past civilizations by analyzing the buildings and relics they left behind—show how the modern world came to be by revealing how it was influenced by the past.

As part of this process, historians and archaeologists try to visualize how the civilizations they study would have appeared hundreds or thousands of years ago. This task can be extremely difficult. Over time, buildings and monuments wear down under the assault of weather, warfare, plant and animal life, and the unending development of younger civilizations. Scholars often have to artistically re-create how ancient structures originally looked, from the design of their roofs to the colors they were painted. The greater the amount of decay or destruction these sites have endured, the harder this task can be.

Fortunately, virtual reality and other high-technology tools are advanced enough to help make this job less burdensome. Over the past few years, researchers have created digital models of ancient churches, palaces, homes, and tombs that either have been damaged or are being threatened by the modern world. So many researchers have become involved in this work, in fact, that they have given it a new name: virtual heritage. For some of these computerized displays, scholars and technicians have built the structures virtual wall by virtual wall, using floor plans drawn up at the site of the original buildings. Other buildings have so many details or are in good enough condition that researchers want to capture images of the actual structures, complete with all the surface details, for their virtual reconstructions.

A couple of methods can yield this level of resolution. In one of the most commonly used techniques, laser scanners bounce low-intensity beams of coherent light across walls, ceilings, and statues to capture extremely small levels of detail, including the texture of the stones or bricks used by the original builders. Another method called photogrammetry can provide enough information to reconstruct buildings that have suffered heavy damage or even have been demolished in recent years. Researchers collect old photographs of the site that were taken from different angles and scan them into graphics computers. By comparing overlapping points on the photos, the researchers can create a close three-dimensional match to the structure's original appearance.

Archaeologists and government officials have been using these techniques to help preserve actual structures as well as to retain virtual models. Two famous stone monuments—the Angkor Wat temple and observatory in Cambodia and Stonehenge in England—have been damaged to varying degrees in the past few decades by the hordes of tourists who visit these sites each year. Though they do not intend to harm these structures, visitors to ancient sites leave behind thousands of acidic fingerprints that eat into the surface of the stone. While each fingerprint does only a tiny amount of damage, the effect of all those prints—as well as the force of all the tourists' footsteps and even the carbon dioxide tourists exhale—combines with normal weathering to wipe away intricate carvings and can weaken building surfaces until they split away.

This type of damage already has claimed much of the surface of Angkor Wat, which dates back to the 1100s and covers a square mile of northwestern Cambodia. Many of the figures that decorate the temple's walls have been worn nearly flat or have broken off over the past decades. To analyze how and where the greatest damage has taken place, scientists created digital maps using old photographs of the site and computer-aided design software that charted the decay rate. With this information, researchers hope to slow or stop the erosion.

At Stonehenge, the ancient ring of gigantic stones in southwest England, officials faced a slightly different problem. Though the gigantic blocks have no decorative carvings, they have coverings of lichen that help protect them against the weather. Once again, tourists' fingerprints were causing problems, this time by killing off the lichen and exposing the stone to the elements. Although Stonehenge is a much-visited site, visitors were banned from getting close enough to touch the stones in an attempt to stop or reverse the damage. However, to avoid disappointing tourists who wanted to take an up-close look at the stones, a British preservation society and a company called Virtual Presence teamed up to create a realistic, highly detailed, three-dimensional model of the site. Visitors could walk through the virtual environment, examine the digitized monoliths, and see how the monument—which experts believe served as an ancient Druidic astronomical observatory—fit into its surroundings, while the real stones recovered from decades of popularity.

Many other ancient structures have been modeled and renovated in digital form. However, some buildings no longer exist at all, except in historical descriptions, while others were stripped of sculptures, wall decorations, and other relics that went to universities and museums around the world. Re-creating these buildings as they were requires a great deal of research and a bit of guesswork, but it is possible. A number of companies, in fact, have created these types of virtual historic environments either as part of their business or as their main area of interest.

Some intriguing work is being done at Learning Sites Inc., which designs virtual learning environments based on ancient archaeological sites. The sites the company has transported into VR range from Egyptian temples and Turkish religious communities to a beekeeper's farmhouse from ancient Greece. The Learning Sites staff takes all the information known about these sites, including the archaeologists' notes, and uses it to create three-dimensional models of the sites as they looked thousands of years ago.

In these interactive displays, visitors can examine how the buildings were put together and how they were decorated and discover for themselves what each room was used for. They can handle computerized representations of objects that archaeologists found when they were excavating the buildings. And they can read notes or listen to brief lectures on how archaeologists discovered the sites and uncovered their treasures. In an early project, a VR restoration of an ancient Egyptian fortress on the Nile River, visitors even had a virtual guide dressed as an Egyptian scribe who took them on a tour of the complex. For a more recent project, the digital renovation of an ancient palace in modern-day Iraq, scholars at the company had to track down images of relics that were scattered among many public and private collections.

Learning Sites, Virtual Presence, and companies that conduct similar work have created other immersive worlds for multiple-user exploration, whether in two-dimensional video kiosks or three-dimensional environment displays. Some of these companies have enhanced their sites on the World Wide Web with VRML samples of the digital environments they create. With appropriate advances in telecommunications technology, people from distant cities or nations may be able to immerse themselves in virtual-reality museum displays, while classes might tour VR archaeology sites with the assistance of the archaeologists who are running the excavation.

16

VR AS A
DESIGN TOOL

Whether they fully immerse their users in a digital landscape or simply make computer graphics seem solid, virtual environments give people the opportunity to see information from a unique perspective. This ability can help people study phenomena that cannot be duplicated in a regular laboratory or learn about times that have long passed away. But it also can benefit people whose work is solidly rooted in the physical world.

Many engineers, commercial designers, and other artisans have been using the tools of virtual reality for years. Digital models of physical objects can be much easier to work with than their real-world counterparts. In digitized form, metal parts that could weigh thousands of pounds can be flipped around with no effort as engineers examine them. Making a change in a complex mechanism can be as simple as deleting an unneeded part or stretching a connector rod to a different length. Also, there are no messes to clean up after the work is finished, not even paint drips to clear away. As a result, virtual reality provides as close to a perfect workshop as anyone who creates tools, machines, and even buildings for a living.

Speeding Up
Vehicle Design

Car design is a collaborative process. The new cars and trucks that appear on dealership parking lots every year are the product of huge planning efforts, ones that involve hundreds of people who spend thousands of hours working together to create vehicles that people will buy. Artists who determine how each car will look and engineers who turn these ideas into construction plans constantly exchange ideas, suggest changes to the design, and agree to compromises between features that are artistically desirable but technically difficult to produce and features that are mechanically possible but aesthetically unpleasing.

At the same time, car designers have to pay close attention to the opinions of potential car buyers. This information comes from many sources, such as comments from car dealers regarding features that people want; news reports on changes in the public's spending habits and lifestyle changes; and surveys of car buyers that car manufacturers themselves conduct. No matter how well its designers think it looks, a car or truck that does not attract people onto a dealership's lot will end up losing money. Considering all these factors requires a lot of flexibility, both from the designers and from the tools they use.

Decades before virtual reality came along, automobile manufacturers were using computer-graphics systems to speed up the process of creating new cars. General Motors Corporation was the first to do so; in fact, their Design Augmented by Computers, or DAC-l, system—which General Motors and IBM designed in the late 1950s—was the first to harness computer power as an aid in drawing industrial plans. Other carmakers picked up the idea, and by the 1980s, most of the work of creating new vehicles involved the use of computer-aided design systems, allowing engineers to create three-dimensional objects—from heavy machinery to houses—on two-dimensional computer displays. (CAD in itself can be seen as a type of semi-virtual reality, as it gives a limited sense of interaction between engineers and their on-screen work.)

However, the process of car design also requires car manufacturers to build full-size prototypes of the cars being developed, as a way to view how the final product would look in a dealership's showroom. Sculptors create clay models of each car's exterior and interior, based on the designers' plans; other workers make full-size fiberglass mock-ups of the car based on these models, creating a complete vehicle body for the automaker's managers to examine and approve for production.

Creating these mock-ups takes time and money, and if enough people object to the design or request too many changes, the whole process has to be repeated. Virtual-reality tools can cut down this phase of car design dramatically. Creating digital models that people can examine and change, a process called *virtual prototyping*, most often involves one of the larger immersive-environment display systems, such as a wall-size screen and shutter glasses. This type of system is best suited for use in a conference room, where each designer can see a life-size image of the proposed vehicle and make changes to the design within minutes.

Large automakers such as General Motors, Ford Motor Company, Mercedes-Benz, and Volvo have used immersive, three-dimensional design systems to create digital prototypes since the middle of the 1990s to create and improve many of their products. General Motors, which designed and used the first CAD system, has used collaborative VR displays in the design of modern vehicles such as its Impala sedan line. Ford used a design system created by a British company, Division Inc., to test planned alterations to its Bronco sport utility truck.

Other vehicle makers have employed immersive design tools as well. In the spring of 1995, Caterpillar Inc., a construction equipment maker, began building a newly redesigned model of its popular line of wheel loaders. This particular loader, the 914G, was different from Caterpillar's previous models. Its rear end sloped away from the operator's cab, making it easier to see what was behind the loader, a welcome change from the squared-off boxes of previous models. The loader's shovel and body also were designed to provide fewer visual obstructions as the operator worked in construction sites.

More remarkably, the new model had gone into production in record time. Caterpillar had started redesigning its loader in the autumn of 1991. Normally, it can take up to seven years to get a new model ready for production, with most of the time taken up by tests of functioning physical prototypes of the new model. The 914G, though, had been prototyped in an early version of the CAVE. The Caterpillar design team controlled a virtual mock-up of the wheel loader with a physical mock-up of the loader's control cab. All of the pedals, levers, and switches were present in the physical cab, as well as on the dashboard of the digitized image of the control cab's interior that appeared on the forward-facing wall of the CAVE.

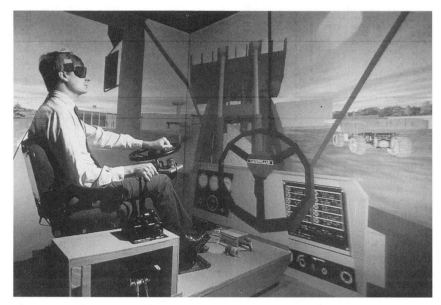

The CAVE environment used to design the 914G wheel loader incorporated a physical reproduction of the machine's controls. The driver is wearing shutter glasses that allow him to perceive the flat computer graphics as a three-dimensional environment. [Courtesy Caterpillar Inc.]

Caterpillar engineers and loader operators "drove" the VR machine around a simulated construction site, moving virtual dirt piles and doing other jobs that the real loader would have to do. Testing alternate designs was simpler in VR than in real life. Rather than build a completely new machine, the engineers simply programmed the changes into the CAVE's computer. Prototyping the loader in VR cut the time it took to produce the final version of the loader to a little over three years, saving Caterpillar millions of dollars.

Virtual Architecture

Architects also use a type of prototyping to demonstrate their building ideas. As with designing vehicles, designing buildings is a complicated process involving hours of planning and drawing. First, the architect comes up with an idea for a building, based on instructions from the building's eventual owners. Next, he or she prepares a model or a drawing of the building, adding in such details as plumbing, air-conditioning, and electrical systems. Finally, the architect presents the idea to other people—the clients, other architects, builders—for evaluation. This process feeds back upon itself, as the architect takes the suggestion he or she received on how to improve the design of the building, changes the plans, and resubmits them for further comment.

Sometimes, the task of translating the idea of how a three-dimensional building should look into two-dimensional blueprints can go awry, creating problems that can be expensive or impossible to fix after construction begins. Floor plans that seem to work on paper can turn out to be difficult to build, inconvenient to walk through, or simply ugly when finished. Architects try to catch these problems before construction begins by building three-dimensional models of the blueprints they create. But these models are too small to let their viewers do anything but imagine what it would be like to stand in the future building. Because these models are small, their viewers can overlook details that are noticeable in a full-size room, such as a door that is too narrow.

Using immersive, interactive virtual environments instead of small-scale physical models can make avoiding these problems easier. Ideally, architects could use immersive graphics, as one researcher said, to "kind of scribble in virtual space just as quickly as he or she can jot down an idea or draw out a napkin sketch." The architect then would be able to expand upon this computerized scribbling, developing full-scale plans and discarding unworkable ideas, without cluttering up his or her workspace with old napkins.

Architects and their clients then could move around the building and interact with the proposed floor plan. They could open doors and windows, walk up and down staircases, and even (in some cases) check how well the building looks compared to nearby buildings. They then could immediately alter the model to test out any changes. Because the original design would be saved in the computer, the architect could undo any changes that turned out to be unnecessary.

Researchers and architects have been experimenting with systems such as this. One of the earliest examples of virtual architecture was the Sitterson Hall project at the University of North Carolina's Chapel Hill campus. The university built Sitterson Hall, which houses the UNC-Chapel Hill computer science department, in the late 1980s. Before construction started, though, some students and research professors took a copy of the architect's blueprints and created a computer

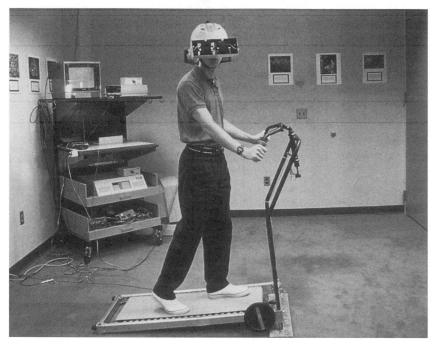

A researcher at the University of North Carolina at Chapel Hill walks through a virtual-reality mock-up of the Sitterson Hall building in the late 1980s. Participants in the early architectural VR experiment used the handlebars on the treadmill to change direction in the digital environment. [Courtesy University of North Carolina at Chapel Hill, Department of Computer Science]

model of the building. They then toured the computerized model, first using a monitor similar to a big-screen television and then using a head-mounted display to see where they were going. A treadmill served as a sort of human-powered mouse, with a sensor on the treadmill telling the computer how far the visitors had walked. A movable set of bicycle handlebars let these virtual-world tourists steer themselves anywhere a person could walk in the real building.

Even though the quality of the display was primitive, the overall effect was good enough for the researchers to see where the building's design needed changing. In one case, the building's architects had placed a low wall between a lobby and a hallway to separate the two areas. While examining their VR model, the researchers discovered that the arrangement made the hallway too narrow. The architects were reluctant to change the design until they saw how it looked in the

VR mock-up. Since the university people were right, the architects moved the wall. Now, the discovery that a wall was out of place is not, in itself, remarkable. The remarkable thing was that the researchers discovered the flaw even though the blueprints indicated that the hallway was wide enough. Without the VR model, the building would have gone up as designed, and the researchers would have had to put up with a cramped hallway.

Since the time the Sitterson Hall walk-through was created, researchers have explored different methods to improve on the techniques used at UNC-Chapel Hill. Their goal has been to create architectural simulations that are as detailed as a real building yet are as easy to rearrange as a set of building blocks.

Detecting Design Flaws with Virtual Reality

Using virtual reality to design buildings also could help architects avoid costly design problems that do not appear until the building goes up. In 1996, a construction firm fought off a lawsuit over a series of leaking roofs in a 64-story office building with the aid of a three-dimensional computer simulation. The top of the building, Two Prudential Plaza in Chicago, looked like a pyramid made up of four staircases resting against one another. Unfortunately, the individual roofs that made up the staircases allowed rainwater to leak inside and drip through the ceilings of the offices below them. The building's owners sued the company that built the tower, Turner Construction, for the cost of repairing the water damage and fixing the roofs. The owners claimed that the company had not followed the blueprints properly when it put up the roofs.

Turner Construction's owners and lawyers knew that the tower had been built according to the plans. But how could they prove that the original roof design had been flawed? And even more important, how could they convince the jury that the original design's flaws, not sloppy construction, caused the leaks? The best way to do all this seemed to be to take the jury on a tour of the original roofs and compare them to the new roofs that the owners had had installed. Turner Construction hired Engineering Applications, a company in Iowa that specialized in engineering simulations, to help prove that the original design had been flawed. Using the original blueprints, Engineering Applications

This image shows how virtual-reality systems could be used to analyze the effects of factory buildings upon nearby communities. [Image courtesy: VR Sim, Inc.]

put together a three-dimensional computer simulation showing how the original design let water find its way into the building. The construction company's lawyers presented the simulation to the jury as a whole on a large two-dimensional monitor. However, the display was detailed enough for the jurors to understand how the original roof structure worked in three dimensions. Combined with other evidence, this simulation convinced the jury in the lawsuit that the construction company was not to blame for the damage caused by the badly designed roofs.

If a two-dimensional presentation of a three-dimensional model is enough to teach a jury about structural engineering, what could trained architects do with a fully immersive model of a planned building? Many architects and VR researchers think that such a system would let architects head off expensive problems, like the one that struck Two Prudential Plaza. A fully immersive virtual building tester also could simplify another problem of architecture: making sure that buildings can weather real-world physical phenomena.

A Virtually Guaranteed Presentation

Along with its current and potential abilities as a design tool, VR can be an impressive vehicle for swaying clients toward approving an architect's ideas. In one case, VR techniques were used to help bring the 1996 Republican presidential nominations to southern California. When the Republican Party began looking for a host city for its national convention, it took bids from such cities as New York, Chicago, New Orleans—and San Diego. Few people thought that San Diego's biggest meeting site, the San Diego Convention Center, could hold all the people expected to attend the nominations. Presidential nominations usually took place in huge convention halls, ones with floors measured in acres and with ceilings up to 70 feet high. In contrast, the San Diego Convention Center had intentionally been designed as a smaller alternative to these larger halls, which because of their size were more expensive to rent. Party officials expected 20,000 to attend the Republican National Convention. The convention center, however, was designed to hold only 12,000 people comfortably.

To show the Republican Party that the convention center was big enough to hold all the delegates, the center officials turned to virtual reality. Specifically, they turned to the San Diego Data Processing Corporation, a nonprofit computing and simulation company owned by the City of San Diego. The company and the convention center created a VR version of the convention center as it might look during the nominations. The model included broadcast platforms for the major TV news organizations, suggested seating for the convention delegates, and a stage and speaker's podium based on one used during the Republicans' 1984 convention. (To appeal to the 1996 convention organizers, the display included a still image of former president Ronald Reagan speaking from the podium and featured signs naming the organizers' home states.) The tour of the proposed convention floor included showing how the convention would look from cameras mounted in various locations and at various heights around the main floor.

Buildings for a Virtual World

There is another way that virtual reality is being combined with the field of architecture, however. Instead of using VR to design buildings for the physical world, some researchers and companies are designing buildings for virtual worlds. In other words, instead of using VR for architecture, they are using VR as architecture.

One of the first applications of virtual architecture has been a series of environments for navigating the World Wide Web, the graphics-heavy subsidiary of the Internet. Working with this globe-spanning network of linked computers has meant having to memorize the long strings of letters, numbers, and arcane symbols that make up Internet and Web addresses or creating search engines that can find and record this information. For years, researchers have tried to develop a more

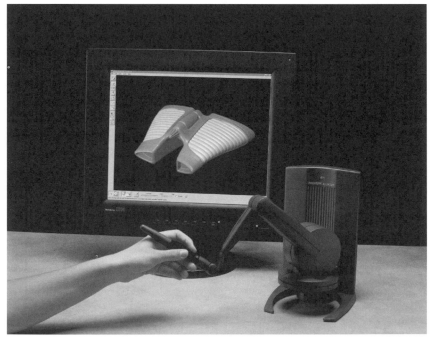

With the proper tools and software, commercial designers can create three-dimensional models of products. (SensAble Technologies)

efficient method for navigating through and interacting with the computerized world.

Dace Campbell, an architect and a former graduate student at the University of Washington's Human Interface Technology Laboratory, made this type of interface the subject of his work. Like other researchers, he believes that using three-dimensional graphics and other sense cues as landmarks would be a better way for on-line explorers to gain access to the data they want. Rather than knowing which codes to enter in a browser's address field, Web users would know in which direction to move their on-line selves once they entered the navigation space. "Virtual architecture, then," Campbell says, "would serve a similar function (to that of physical architecture) except it's composed of polygons and vertices and texture maps, as opposed to bricks and mortar and steel."

A few companies have tried to put these theories into practice over the few years that the Web has been in existence. One company, a Canadian firm called antarcti.ca, took a creative approach, dividing a map of the continent of Antarctica into a series of territories devoted to different categories of websites. By selecting categories and subcategories, Web surfers eventually reached virtual villages that provided the needed information. Each building in the village was a link to a separate website; the size and shape of the building indicated if it linked to a corporation, a university, or simply a hobbyist's private information site.

Comfort and Convenience, Courtesy of VR

Virtual prototyping is not limited to simulating the mechanics of a product. It also can account for the comfort and convenience of the people who use that product, be it an automobile or a factory workspace. *Ergonomics*, the art of designing products that are comfortable to use, is a very exacting field. Engineers use body measurements taken from hundreds of people to sculpt equipment controls and build seats and work areas that conform to their human users. Experimenting with ergonomic mock-ups is a lengthy and expensive process, as is building machinery prototypes. And, as with VR machinery prototypes, adjusting ergonomic layouts in VR can save a great deal of time and money.

To do this, designers use computerized human figures that are rendered at the same scale as the equipment or spaces being designed.

These figures, which generally are known as "manikins," can be as simple or as detailed as their users require. Designers can place these manikins on a truck's driver seat, for example, to see if there is enough space between the figure's knees and the steering wheel. These figures also can serve as stand-ins for mechanics as engineers evaluate how easy it is to reach and work on the truck's machinery.

Manikins also can serve as digital puppets when they are controlled by designers using force-feedback manipulators or other effectors. This type of setup allows the designers to actively explore how well a real person might be able to work with a machine or in a particular workspace.

VR AS A
HEALING TOOL

Some of the most dramatic adaptations of virtual reality to real-life tasks have occurred in the field of medicine. Surgeons are developing and using computer tools to test out medical procedures before their patients enter the hospital. Therapists are using simulations to show people with a range of physical handicaps how to function ably in the everyday world. Even psychiatrists have been able to use VR to help people confront and overcome their deepest fears in controlled virtual environments.

VR gives medical practitioners the ability to do risky work safely and practice complicated tasks until they gain proficiency. In fact, virtual environments based on the human body already are being developed to teach medical students some of the basics of their field. Learning the anatomy of the human body, how all these structures and tissues fit and work together, is an overwhelming task. Even though the human body is a three-dimensional structure, medical students learn this structure mainly by studying two-dimensional charts and medical textbook illustrations. Schools provide human skeletons and physical models of various sections of the body for study, but these are costly resources. Skeletons can cost from a few hundred to a few thousand dollars, and a useful model of just part of the upper body easily can cost the same.

Virtual reality's ability to mimic the appearance of three-dimensional structures offers a cheaper and more useful alternative. A number of databases already feature two-dimensional cross sections of entire human bodies, and the organizations that maintain these databases have been adapting them for three-dimensional displays. One of the most well known of these collections is the Visible Human database at the University of Colorado School of Medicine, which contains photos of 1-millimeter-wide (1/25-inch-wide) cross sections of human cadavers. This information already is being used in conventional computer programs that teach anatomy, and researchers at the university have used images from the database to create experimental surgical simulators.

Surgical Simulations

To apply his or her surgical knowledge successfully, a surgeon has to have had at least some experience in operating on the human body. However, practicing on living human bodies is out of the question. Learning to operate on cadavers is a common practice, but dead bodies simply do not act the same way living bodies do when cut open. What is worse, once a cadaver has been "operated" on, there is no way to undo the work and give another surgeon-in-training a fresh start.

This is where virtual reality can make a big difference. Dissections conducted with digital reconstructions of human bodies—especially ones programmed to bleed and otherwise act as would a real body— would be as realistic a simulation as could be asked for. It also would be reusable, as the simulation could be reset once a student finished dissecting it. The simulation would also be easier to care for. Cadavers have to be preserved with special chemicals and stored in refrigerated vaults to keep them from decaying. A VR re-creation of a human body, on the other hand, would only need a computer with sufficient storage space.

Immersive computer systems that simulate complex surgical procedures are even more useful. All forms of surgery put patients at risk, from simple procedures like wart removal to lengthy operations that involve teams of surgeons. Cutting into the body in order to heal it can pose many dangers, even with the high quality of modern medical care. Patients can react badly to anesthetics; organs can turn out to be more seriously damaged or diseased than tests indicated; surgeons even can discover problems that did not appear on X rays or other tests. Each operation is unique, and each patient responds to treatment differently. Surgeons need a great deal of practice to handle all these variables.

Airplane pilots do not fly solo until they have flown a certain number of hours under an instructor's supervision. Likewise, new surgeons do not operate on patients without going through an apprenticeship called a residency. They first observe and assist experienced surgeons. They then perform operations while an experienced surgeon observes them. Only after being certified as competent does a surgeon begin to operate on his or her own. Even then, surgeons have to prepare for each operation with great care and keep themselves trained in up-to-date surgical techniques.

Practicing ways to handle surgical situations is a task well suited for virtual reality. By feeding details of a patient's condition into a surgical simulator, surgeons can try out a variety of treatments, discarding ones that did not work and correcting any mistakes. In this manner, surgeons can eliminate much of the uncertainty that accompanies any operation.

Creating virtual environments that can reproduce the visual and physical sensations of surgery has been a difficult task to accomplish, though. Aside from the software that accurately controls such simulations, the main need is for a reliable way to simulate the feel of surgery in virtual reality. The human body is an incredibly complex system of organs, blood vessels, muscles, bones, and other conglomerations of living cells. Each of these tissues feels different under the surgeon's scalpel, and each can respond differently during an operation.

Some researchers have tried to incorporate the feel of surgery through force-feedback tools. The inventor of the PHANTOM haptic effector, Thomas Massie, developed a virtual environment that mimicked a procedure called a needle biopsy, which physicians use to remove small pieces of tumors or other diseased organs for examination without opening a hole in the patient's body. Massie's program simulated a needle biopsy for extracting samples of brain tumors, using a strong needle that passes through the skull and into the brain until it reaches the tumor. In the simulation, the attempt to drive the on-screen needle into the virtual patient's head met with varying degrees of resistance, reproducing the feel of a needle poking through the scalp, the skull, and various layers of brain tissue.

For the past few years, the University of Colorado's Center for Human Simulation has been using PHANTOMs to create other types of surgical training simulators. In one version, researchers have paired a force-feedback scalpel with a computerized model of the human leg to show the proper method for starting a knee operation. The simulator provides the sensation of cutting through skin and fat layers to expose muscles, bones, and other structures beneath the surface.

In general, though, few of these surgical simulators have made the transition from the laboratory to actual use in medical schools and hospitals. Despite years of improvement in computer technology, virtual-reality tools still are too expensive for most hospitals to afford, and the quality of most simulations still is too primitive to be of much use. However, the current techniques of virtual reality are well suited for some operations.

Although surgery involves cutting into the human body, surgeons strive to do the fewest incisions necessary to fix whatever is wrong. In the past few decades, surgeons have relied on *endoscopic* ("inside view") surgery, also known as keyhole surgery, as an alternative to opening up large areas of the body. Making smaller incisions does less damage to the body and ultimately speeds up a patient's recovery time. One of the most well-known forms of keyhole surgery is *arthroscopic* knee surgery (arthroscopic means "looking at the joint"), which often is performed on professional athletes. Another common keyhole operation is *laparoscopy*, which involves operating inside the chest or abdomen.

In a laparoscopy, the surgeon inserts his or her instruments into the body through *trocars*, tubes with a one-way gasket on the end that stays outside the body. One of the tools the surgeon uses combines a tiny video camera and optical-fiber lights to send images of the operation to a two-dimensional video monitor. Watching the screen, the surgeon manipulates surgical instruments that are inserted through other trocars. The major drawback to keyhole surgery is that surgeons cannot see exactly what they are doing. They navigate through the body and operate on the body by looking at images of the operation site, not by looking at the site itself. This is a hard technique to master, and a surgeon who is learning how to perform these operations can unintentionally hurt a patient. A number of keyhole operations have gone wrong simply because the surgeons could not find the operation site or because they lost track of where their instruments were.

Virtual-reality techniques are helping surgeons shorten this learning period by reproducing the combination of two- and three-dimensional cues that exist in current keyhole surgery. As the students go through a series of increasingly more difficult simulations, experienced surgeons can track how well the students are learning the techniques.

Students use the handles of actual laparoscopic instruments to manipulate three-dimensional shapes or representations of actual joints and organs in a three-dimensional surgical environment. These simulators can incorporate three-dimensional goggles to display these images, though some lower-priced systems use high-resolution, two-dimensional monitors. Because surgeons often conduct real-world endoscopic operations using two-dimensional monitors, they do not require fully immersive displays while training.

Virtual-reality techniques have been used in more dramatic forms of surgery. In spring 2001, a team of surgeons in Singapore separated two baby girls who had been joined at the skull when they were born. Separating conjoined twins (also known as Siamese twins, after a famous pair of conjoined twins from Asia) is a very difficult procedure, especially in cases where the twins share major organs or structures such as the skull. Many times, physicians will decide not to put their patients through the risky ordeal. But the surgeons who separated the girls in Singapore had an extra tool to prepare for the operation: a virtual-reality simulator that had been created at the National University of Singapore with assistance from Johns Hopkins University Hospital in Baltimore, Maryland. Called VizDExter, the simulator displayed a clear stereoscopic image of the girls' fused skull and each of their brains, allowing the surgeons to plan exactly where they would separate the girls.

Virtual Operating Rooms

There is a difference between applying knowledge gained in virtual reality to a real-life operation and using virtual reality as an aid *in* a real-life operation. Even the best VR surgery simulator, one that could provide a three-dimensional view of the patient, would be useful only while the surgeon was learning his or her techniques or preparing for an operation. A better system would allow surgeons to look at three-dimensional images of their patients *during* the operation, especially during endoscopic or other operations in very tight spaces.

As it happens, surgeons have come very close to using such systems in real life. Starting in the last half of the 1990s, a few surgeons began conducting long-distance operations by controlling the movements of surgical robots from control rooms that were hundreds, or even thousands, of miles from their patients. Called telerobotics, this method of connecting surgeons to patients is being explored as a way to provide sophisticated medical care to people who live far from major medical centers. From 1996 to 2001, surgeons used experimental telerobotic systems to remove gall bladders, perform groin surgery, and treat varicose veins over phone lines and satellite hookups connecting cities on opposite sides of the planet. Though the surgeons who performed these operations used two-dimensional monitors to observe the procedures, researchers hope to add three-dimensional displays in the future.

Immersive computing in the operating room also could include the use of augmented reality, which projects computer-generated images over views of the real world. Most of the research being done with augmented reality is designed to help mechanics and technicians build and repair machines. Some augmented-reality research, however, has focused on opening a "magic window" in the side of patients on the operating table. Such a system could combine data from ultrasound, X ray, or other types of scans and project them onto a see-through display screen, showing surgeons exactly where they need to guide their instruments.

Physical Therapy in a Virtual World

Unfortunately, many maladies cannot be cured either by surgery or by medication. Phobias are extreme fears of things (such as spiders) or situations (such as riding in elevators). The word *phobia* itself is a Greek word that means "fear." Some people develop phobias as the result of traumatic events. Falling off a tall jungle gym on a playground, for instance, can cause a child to develop a lifelong fear of heights, or *acrophobia*. Other people develop phobias for no apparent reason; such phobias can include the fear of flying or even the fear of being outdoors.

Some people fight their phobias with months or years of psychological analysis, medication or relaxation techniques to reduce anxiety, and gradual immersion therapy that slowly exposes that person to the object of his or her fear. Other people can take a more drastic approach, such as overcoming acrophobia by jumping off a high diving board into a swimming pool. A number of researchers have been using virtual reality to provide a comfortable middle ground between these two extremes.

"Spider World" is a virtual environment designed to help people who are scared of spiders fight their fear. Patients encounter virtual spiders and 3-D spiderwebs in the comparative safety of a computer-generated kitchen. Therapists also use a furry toy spider to give phobics the sensation of touching virtual spiders. This "mixed reality" technique adds to the realism of the VR display. [Courtesy Human Interface Technology Laboratory]

Acrophobia, the fear of heights, lends itself very easily to virtual-reality simulations. Using virtual architecture techniques, therapists can create environments that reproduce, and even exaggerate, the visual cues that trigger acrophobia. The first study in using VR therapy to treat acrophobia took place in Atlanta, Georgia, when a computing professor at the Georgia Institute of Technology and a psychiatry professor at Emory University designed a computer-generated high-rise hotel lobby, complete with a glass-walled elevator. The professors, Larry Hodges and Barbara Rothbaum, introduced their test subjects to the environment at ground level, giving them the opportunity to look around and see how tall the virtual hotel actually was. Then the subjects entered the elevator and gradually traveled to higher floors, until they were able to step out of the elevator onto the top-floor balcony and look down at the lobby's floor. The two researchers went on to develop successful treatment environments for people who were afraid to fly and for veterans of the Vietnam War who suffer from posttraumatic stress disorder, repeatedly reliving their combat experiences.

A few years later, a California researcher, Dr. Ralph Lemson of the Kaiser-Permanente Medical Group's Department of Psychiatry, developed another particularly terrifying scenario. His environment showed a café patio, complete with a black-and-white tile floor and umbrella-shaded tables, hanging in midair over San Francisco Bay, with a plank leading to a representation of the Golden Gate Bridge. Volunteers who suffered from acrophobia donned head-mounted displays and were asked to step onto the patio, walk over the plank, and stroll around on the bridge.

Dr. Lemson and his assistants monitored the volunteers' heart rate and blood pressure while the tests were going on, as well as talking to

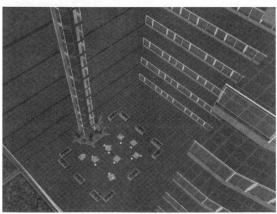

Another phobia that has been treated using virtual-reality therapy is acrophobia, the fear of heights. In environments such as this shopping mall food court/atrium, patients are exposed to gradually increasing heights within a building, starting at ground level (phobia1) and eventually reaching the uppermost floors (phobia2). [Image courtesy: www.5dt.com]

the volunteers and asking how they felt. The simulation caused the same reactions in the volunteers—shortness of breath, vertigo, and anxiety—that they felt in the real world. However, the ability to step away from the virtual environment helped the volunteers to withstand the simulation for gradually longer periods. Once they were comfortable with the virtual environment, the volunteers went on to meet real-world challenges that included driving across a bridge and riding up a building inside a glass elevator.

The success of this type of virtual therapy can be seen by the results of the first series of tests Dr. Lemson conducted. Thirty-two of Dr. Lemson's patients participated in the virtual environment. Of these people, all but two or three were able to overcome their fear of heights in the real world. Other researchers studying the use of VR as a phobia fighter have reported similar results. At the University of Washington's HIT Lab, a virtual environment called SpiderWorld has helped people overcome their extreme fear of spiders by exposing them to increasingly scary arachnids in a virtual kitchen that comes complete with spiderwebs. Central to the experience is getting the test subjects to look at and touch a computer-generated tarantula with oversize fangs.

VR therapy also can be used to help people handle disabilities that are even more serious. At the Oregon Research Institute in Eugene, Oregon, Dr. Dean Inman has developed a virtual environment that can help people learn how to use wheelchairs. Inman's program is similar to the project that shows how to adapt building plans for those who are wheelchair-bound. Where the architectural simulator passively monitors how many times the wheelchair wheels turned, though, the ORI project actively controls how the wheelchair acts in the virtual environment. The wheelchair sits on a platform rigged to give feedback through the wheels of the chair. Steering the chair through the simulation with a joystick, the user can sense how it feels to ride over smooth sidewalks, rough dirt paths, and patches of ice. The simulator also lets the user steer through different rooms that range from spacious to cluttered and even provides training in off-road navigation with a virtual grass-covered hill.

Feeling Virtually No Pain

Virtual-reality therapy can help people bear up to pain as successfully as it can help them overcome their deepest fears. Although pain is triggered by damage to the body, the way a person reacts to pain often depends on how much attention he or she devotes to the pain. People often can ignore a low amount of pain by reading, watching television, or doing other things to take their minds off their discomfort. With sufficient distraction, people can overcome even moderate amounts of pain.

Throughout the 1990s and into the early 2000s, VR researchers throughout the world have created immersive environments that tapped into the ability to distract patients from focusing on pain. Researchers in Japan, Italy, and elsewhere have used virtual-reality therapy to help cancer patients handle the pain of their disease and to relax during chemotherapy and other forms of treatment. Other projects have concentrated on helping people withstand minor, but painful, surgical procedures in which physicians and therapists use little, if any, anesthesia. Burn victims also fall into this category and were some of the first patients to be helped with VR therapy.

To help their bodies heal and return their muscles to a full range of motion, burn victims have to endure a great deal of pain. The bandages covering their burns have to be changed every day, exposing raw skin to painful levels of stimulation. Physical therapy to stretch and rebuild skin and muscle tissue created additional amounts of agony. Painkillers can blunt some of the pain, but the damage often is so extensive that only an extremely powerful drug can block all feeling. And, unfortunately, such drugs usually leave patients unable to take part in the therapy they need.

Here is where VR therapy can play a role. In Seattle, researchers from the University of Washington's HIT Lab gave some burn victims the opportunity to take part in a simple immersive environment— essentially, the same one created for SpiderWorld—to supplement the normal amounts of pain-killing drugs they took before going through a short session of physical therapy. Each session lasted only three minutes, but the patients reported feeling far less pain and discomfort when they used the VR equipment than when they did the same amount of therapy without it. These results encouraged the UW researchers to develop immersive programs that provide a deeper level of distracting interaction, one of which will allow burn patients to fly through an icy canyon and lob snowballs at snowmen.

18

DEVELOPING VR AS
A BUSINESS

The researchers and inventors who brought virtual reality into being hoped it would become a widespread "technology of the future." They had ample reason to believe people would want to invest in and start using virtual environments. The public already was becoming used to having personal computers on office desktops, making calls on portable telephones, and sending documents across town or across the country on fax machines. It seemed as if the technology of VR would be the next logical step in the development of computers. Though the first VR systems were expensive and provided very simple levels of immersion, they sparked hopes for a new and excitingly futuristic wave of development.

Virtual reality was a good subject for publicity as well, with its ability to draw people into digital dimensions of computer data. The news media—television news programs in particular—as well as science-fiction television shows and movies showed images of VR systems in use, bringing the idea of the technology, if not the substance, to the public's attention. People were captivated by the apparent wonders of virtual reality and the ability to work inside the computer. VR researchers helped push the idea of VR themselves, but the initial wave of enthusiasm pretty much sustained itself.

Before long, unfortunately, the enthusiasm *for* virtual reality had outstripped the capability *of* virtual reality to live up to these expectations. The public discovered that, outside of some video arcades and special virtual-reality centers, most VR systems were restricted to university campuses, research institutions, and large corporations that were trying to improve the still-developing technology. Aside from those used in video games and design work, virtual environments generally were devoted to showing how virtual environments might be used when the technology improved enough. And, above all other problems, good VR systems cost a lot of money to put together. The news media and the public gradually lost interest in VR by the late 1990s, though researchers, engineers, and other users kept on improving the technology.

At the beginning of the 21st century, virtual reality was a small part of the world of computing. CyberEdge Information Services, a company that monitors and reports on the visual-simulation industry—including virtual reality—publishes a yearly report called *The Market for Visual Simulation/Virtual Reality Systems*. In the 2001 edition of this report, the firm said there were more than 8,500 companies and organizations around the world working in visual simulation in some way and said the field as a whole was worth more than $22 billion. By itself, that amount may seem like a lot of money, but it is just a fraction of the trillions of dollars earned by the entire computer industry every year. The virtual-environment industry spent a lot of time and effort to get where they are today, and the technology still has a long way to go before it lives up to its potential.

VR Enters the Business World

At the end of the 1980s, virtual reality was an experimental computing tool found only in research laboratories and a few small companies. For VR to flourish, it had to make the same jump to the public marketplace that computers had made decades before. Some of the first commercially produced electronic computers came from companies founded or assisted by the researchers who pioneered these thinking machines. For example, J. Presper Eckert and John Mauchly—the University of

Pennsylvania engineers who designed and assembled ENIAC—formed the Eckert & Mauchly Computer Corporation after World War II and built one of the most famous of the early computer systems: the Universal Automatic Computer, or UNIVAC. They later sold their company to Remington Rand, an office equipment manufacturer that became the Sperry Rand Corporation. IBM, the world's biggest office machine manufacturer and the company that built the 51-foot-long Automatic Sequence Controlled Calculator, soon began building electronic computers of its own, as did other companies and institutions that took part in World War II–era computer projects.

Likewise, the first companies to make virtual-reality systems got into the business through their connections to the first virtual-reality projects. One of the earliest of these firms was Evans & Sutherland Computer Corporation, whose founders, Dave Evans and Ivan Sutherland, were pioneers in computer graphics and immersive computing. They formed their company in 1968 to make graphics computers for flight simulators; over time, the company expanded into other areas of computer graphics, including virtual reality. Later, the companies that contributed components to NASA's VIEW claimed a large share of territory in the new virtual-environment industry. VPL Research, the small company that supplied the wired glove used by VIEW researchers, began selling the first complete VR systems. Silicon Graphics Inc., which built the graphics workstations that generated the simulations, and Autodesk, a CAD software company that designed the three-dimensional imaging programs VIEW used, went on to become leaders in their areas.

But the researchers who pioneered and promoted the idea of immersive computing also knew how much work still needed to be done on the emerging tools of VR. They realized that the computers they used had to be faster, the head-mounted displays had to be less bulky, and the other hardware and software tools had to be improved as well. They also realized that these improvements would come about only when enough people bought and used VR systems to justify the cost of making these improvements.

Some university VR researchers left the academic world and formed their own companies to build and sell the technology they had helped develop, as Evans and Sutherland had. Others decided to promote VR technology from within the university system, establishing connections between researchers and companies that might be interested in their projects. Universities often encourage these types of arrangements, and many have special divisions that do nothing but form and maintain these academic-to-business links. Such connections benefit all sides that take part in the exchange: researchers gain extra support for their projects, universities benefit from licensing fees they charge companies to develop and sell the technology, and companies can offer new products without spending the time and effort to create them from scratch.

The experience of Thomas Furness, the air force researcher who headed the VCASS/SuperCockpit project, is a good example of how such projects get started. When news of the project reached the public, people all around the country began calling Furness to ask about nonmilitary uses for the technology. As he answered these callers' questions, Furness began wondering if there might not be a way to turn his work into something that could benefit anyone who wanted to use computers, not just pilots seeking to improve their skills. After a few months, he came up with a plan to leave his military research work and establish a technological research group to support independent investigations of immersive computing techniques.

"The bottom line of my plan was that we needed to get it out of the military, and I proposed to set up a laboratory somewhere in the U.S. that would work on getting the technology out," Furness said.

After taking a year to identify the most likely uses for VR and refining his ideas for the laboratory, Furness began offering his plan to universities across the nation that might want to sponsor it. Eventually, Furness established his Human Interface Technology Laboratory in 1989 at the University of Washington in Seattle, as part of the school's Washington Technology Center. Seattle seemed to be an ideal spot for the HIT Lab and its goal for improving computer technology. It was, and still is, a center for high-technology research and manufacturing: Microsoft Corporation and many smaller software firms were located nearby, and the Boeing Company, which already was interested in the work Furness was doing, had both its headquarters and its airplane assembly plant on the south side of the city. Having this existing technology base helped Furness attract researchers, instructors, and students to the HIT Lab. There, they were able to develop new methods of immersive computing and use this knowledge to form companies that would bring VR to the marketplace.

From 1989 to 2001, the laboratory served as the hatching ground for 21 hardware and software companies—including one that Furness and some colleagues formed to sell head-mounted displays shaped like large eyeglasses or visors. It also served as the organizing body behind the Virtual Worlds Consortium, an organization for companies and research laboratories involved in immersive computing. Perhaps the most amazing thing about the HIT Lab, though, is its size. A little more than 120 people worked there in 2001, some of them students pursuing their college degrees, others professors conducting their own research while they teach.

HIT Lab is one of many similar groups spread out around the world, all of which seek to improve the state of VR technology and bring it to the marketplace. So why is there so little news about the work of these groups and of the VR systems already in use? Part of the answer to that question could be because there was a little *too much* news about VR when it first came out.

Cyberhype: Mistaking Possibilities for Predictions

Unfortunately, when an innovative new technology such as virtual reality comes along, people often do not distinguish between what it *might* be able to do and what it truly *can* do. Throughout its early years, virtual reality was presented to the world as being more advanced and easier to use that it really was. Newspaper articles, magazine features, and TV reports about VR focused on the great technological advance it represented. Never before, without resorting to full-scale models, had anything come as close to replicating the sensations of the physical world. But media reports paid far less attention to the problems VR researchers had to solve, such as low picture resolution in HMDs and long lag times between a user's actions and their effect upon the virtual environment.

As a result, many people who were not directly involved in the field developed a falsely optimistic impression of VR. The publicity showed VR as cutting-edge technology, which it was, and laser sharp, which it was not. In the real world, VR generally was expensive, finicky, and slow. Some systems provided amazingly realistic experiences, but these generally were designed for special displays of VR's potential, rather than for run-of-the-mill tasks. Typically, VR effectors took a lot of getting used to, and they displayed images that were primitive and hard to see. Once people became used to the display, they found that much of the content was interesting without being astounding. Even some advanced environments were not as useful on a day-to-day basis as the word processors and spreadsheet programs that turned personal computers into office machines.

Virtual-reality companies can create amazingly realistic reproductions of exhilarating experiences. Many of these experiences, however, have been created as demonstration projects to show the capabilities of advanced VR systems, or as special-purpose entertainment environments. Because affordable, everyday VR applications could not provide comparable levels of detail, many people became disillusioned with the technology. [Evans & Sutherland Computer Corp.]

A former HIT Lab student—Dace Campbell, the architect mentioned in chapter 16—discovered that the image VR being poised to change the future of computing was far different from the technology he started using in 1993. "I came to the lab and found that the technology isn't anywhere near where I thought it was," he says. "And so I spent a lot of my time writing and trying to organize more the ways [people and VR systems] can interact than actually making them interact."

Researchers such as Campbell understood that VR needed to be improved, but they also believed that the technology eventually *would* do all the things they said it might do, or at least come very close. It would take awhile before the technology reached retail stores, but it would arrive—eventually.

"One of the frustrating things for me as a researcher is that the media often portrays technology as being 'here,' 'now,' 'today.' And that's dangerous, because people get 'there' and it whets their appetites a little bit, and then they understand just how far away it is and they walk away disappointed and frustrated. So it's very easy, I think, for the media to capture an idea that *will* come and say that it's already here," Campbell said.

"That whole process, from laboratory to store, is very long, with many stages," said Dr. Ulrich Neumann, Director of the Integrated Media Systems Center, a National Science Foundation–funded engineering research center at the University of Southern California, which also sponsors research into virtual-environment technology and connects it with potential corporate backers. "Hype always has a way of getting ahead of that process, because it's so easy to forget how difficult those processes are. Hype is easy because it's just writing, or just telling a story about what could be possible without really examining the details."

This storytelling can be harmful when the story is about a technological advance that works well in the laboratory or during limited demonstrations, yet needs further development before it is ready for widespread use. "It's like a presentation tool, but often people run with it, let their minds and imaginations go," Neumann said. "And, maybe, sometimes scientists are at fault, too, in that they fail to remind people to put the brakes on this kind of runaway enthusiasm."

Though the enthusiasm over what VR might do had gone beyond what it could do in the middle of the 1990s, many people felt that the technology was to blame for not living up to the hype. At the same time, another new computer technology was capturing media and public attention. The World Wide Web was far less expensive than VR and was far easier to use. People could find information or exchange e-mail simply by adding a modem and signing up with a company that connected them to the Internet. Many people and companies have tried combining the Web with VR techniques, in particular with a group of three-dimensional programming techniques generally known as Virtual Reality Modeling Language, but sites that make use of this tool have been slow to catch on. On-line communities and 3-D game sites have attracted a few hundred thousand users, but the majority of people on the Web use, and are satisfied with, its two-dimensional features.

On the other hand, noted HIT Lab founder Tom Furness, while hype can be harmful in raising false expectations, it also can help draw attention to and long-term interest in new discoveries.

"I believe that hype is important, because it excites people, motivates people, and causes support to unfold for investment in these things," Furness said. "Now, what usually happens, and will probably always will happen, is what (in this case) I call the VR winter, after the hype is over and people find out 'this isn't *that* great.'"

Virtual reality has survived during its winter years because enough people believe in its potential to use it in its current form and improve it to the point where it may be able to meet its creators' early expectations.

The VR Market Today

If the hype surrounding the early years of VR was not all bad, neither was it completely hype. The word *hype* is a shortened form of "hyperbole" (pronounced "hy-PER-bah-lē"), which means to overexaggerate the importance of a thing or an event. Despite its limitations, virtual reality was and is an important step forward in making computers easier for people to use. The fact that so many people have found so many ways to use VR shows how well the technology can perform.

There have been plenty of setbacks along the way, of course, aside from the hype-induced disappointment. Many companies that produced VR equipment either have gone out of business or were taken over by other companies. (In fact, VPL Research, the first commercial VR firm, suffered both fates in the early 1990s. Two companies that had loaned money to VPL took control of the company in 1993, but quietly shut it down a few years later after it failed to earn a profit.) A technology boom in the 1990s that pulled the public's attention to the World Wide Web and the following "technology crash" of 2000–2001, in which many high-technology companies declined or went out of business, had an effect on the VR industry as well. Companies that had been known as major VR gaming or research systems as little as three years before declared bankruptcy, split into smaller companies, or switched their business to non-VR fields, such as software development or equipment sales.

VR still makes its presence felt in the world of consumer electronics, though. VR-influenced toys keep appearing on store shelves, from simple games such as LCD baseball video games built into stubby, motion-sensing baseball bats to HMDs that are combined with stationary snowboards or skateboards to create the impression of shredding down a mountainside or surfing a sidewalk far from home. Serious tools also seemingly have roots in virtual-environment research: At the 2001 Comdex consumer-electronics trade show in Las Vegas, the award for "Best New Technology" went to a Swedish firm that was developing a boardless "keyboard" for handheld computers. A set of sensors on the back of the user's hands kept track of finger movements; when users "typed" on a tabletop or in midair, the sensors determined which keys they would have pressed on a real keyboard.

In general, though, most people come across virtual-environment technology through video games. Some large arcade-style games immerse players in three-dimensional, sight-and-sound environments, either with HMDs and other effectors or with fully enclosed gaming cockpits that display battlefields or racetracks on 3-D view screens. Others use less immersive methods of interaction, such as combining a stereoscopic display with standard joystick controls.

There have been quite a few options over the years for gamers who want to bring VR into their homes. Inexpensive VR equipment has been around since 1989. The Mattel PowerGlove, mentioned earlier, was a VR glove controller that was manufactured for the Nintendo Entertainment System video-game player. It was based on the VPL Research DataGlove, but used plastic strips covered with metallic ink rather than optical fibers to monitor how the fingers flexed. A game control panel on the back of the glove allowed users to fully interact with regular games and with the games designed especially for the glove. A transducer on the back of the glove emitted ultrasonic pulses that were picked up by a receiver that attached to the NES unit, allowing the system to track the glove. The glove was a big seller for Mattel. It was popular not just with video gamers but also with VR system builders who saw it as a cheap alternative to the more expensive gloves that used fiber optics or other devices to measure finger positions. The PowerGlove was not as accurate as these other gloves, but at under $100 a pair it was a hard deal to beat.

Other virtual-reality gaming gear came on the market as the 1990s progressed. Nintendo, seeing the popularity of the PowerGlove, developed a goggle-style stereoscopic display called the Virtual Boy. It was fairly unsophisticated compared to full-scale HMDs: It displayed games in just one color—red—and was attached to a tripod that rested on a tabletop. To use it, gamers had to position themselves so their face was even with the goggles and then hold their head steady during game play. Even so, it was the only low-priced VR display available for a year or two.

These days, there are more options for at-home VR. Shutter glasses, combined with the appropriate graphics hardware and software, can give images on standard two-dimensional monitors the illu-

sion of depth. Force-feedback joysticks and steering wheels can re-create the sensations of flying through heavy midair combat or driving a
dune buggy across a desert. Hearing where things are is simply a matter of installing the right sound card and speaker system. And, as computer technology improves in the coming years, the number and type
of immersive experiences people can take part in should increase as
well.

DRAWBACKS TO VR

Mimicking the physical world with computers and innovative effectors turned out to be a goal that was easy to set and difficult to attain. For most of its first two decades, virtual reality provided a choice between two unsatisfactory alternatives. Systems that created fast, accurate, and realistic experiences were too expensive for most people to afford, while budget-level VR setups provided limited levels of interaction in mostly cartoonish environments. As the most fervent supporters of immersive computing would admit, their work in the 1980s and 1990s were just baby steps on the path to the technology they hoped VR would become. Even though it had been in existence for roughly 15 years, virtual reality still was a technology under construction by the beginning of the 21st century.

During this time, people who developed and used VR discovered problems that were more serious than slow refresh rates or inaccurate hand-position calculations. VR users found themselves responding physically to the virtual world—getting dizzy and nauseous while working with the environment, becoming disoriented following their "return" to the real world after finishing a session, developing muscle strains and cramps from using the equipment. Pilots who trained in flight simulators knew about some of these problems, because they had experienced them during their training. But few people outside the military and the civilian aviation world had ever interacted with computers exactly this way before. Even the researchers who knew about the problems pilots encountered did not know exactly what to expect from VR.

As it turned out, fooling the brain into interpreting computer-generated images as real-world phenomena was a far more risky feat than anyone imagined. Inserting people into a virtual environment creates side effects that are as potent as those of some prescription medications or even some illegal drugs. Researchers have discovered that VR experiences can even rewire the brain, temporarily altering the way people perceive the real world around them. Many researchers today still are searching for ways to resolve this clash between the computer-generated and the real worlds.

Cyberspace Sickness

When we move, our bodies register more sensations than just the change of view. Our muscles signal the brain that they are moving and in which direction they are doing most of their work. Skin cells sense the slight breeze created as we swing our arms and legs, and the changes of temperature as we move into and out of the sun. We usually do not notice these signals unless we concentrate on them or unless the pain from a bruise or a pulled muscle draws our attention. Otherwise, these signals become part of the background noise of our bodies.

Another current in this stream of signals flowing through our bodies is made up of positioning messages the various parts of the body send to the brain. *Proprioception* is the body's sense of its own movement that comes from special nerve cells—called, appropriately, proprioceptors—in the muscles, the bones, the joints, and the skin. This sense allows the brain to keep track of where each part of the body is in relation to all of its other parts. The brain uses this information to coordinate all the large- and small-muscle movement needed to stand upright, walk in straight lines, balance in awkward positions without falling over, and do just about everything else.

Along with the proprioceptors that tell where each part of the body is in relation to all the others, we carry position trackers on each side of our head that tell us where we are in relation to the rest of the world.

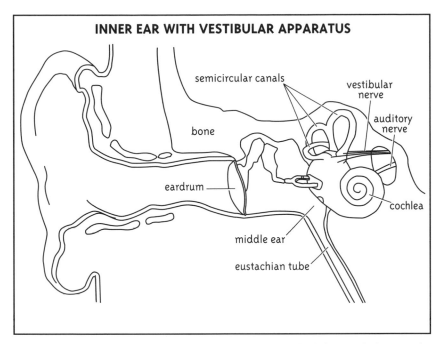

INNER EAR WITH VESTIBULAR APPARATUS

semicircular canals

vestibular nerve

auditory nerve

bone

eardrum

cochlea

middle ear

eustachian tube

Part of the inner ear, the vestibular apparatus acts as the body's main balance and positioning sensor.

Our inner ears contain a number of motion-sensing organs, including one called the *vestibular apparatus* that gives us our sense of balance. The vestibular apparatus is made up of three fluid-filled tubes, called the semicircular canals, that make horizontal and vertical loops. As our heads move, the fluid shifts around, triggering nerve cells that send signals about this movement to the brain.

These signals, combined with other information from the inner ears, help us keep our balance and contribute to the sense of acceleration and deceleration when we move. The signals also help control a phenomenon called the *vestibular-ocular reflex*, the automatic adjustment that the eye muscles make to keep our view of the world stable as we move and look around.

In some people, these processes malfunction. The inner ears can send movement signals when a person is not moving or not send the proper signals when that person *is* moving. Such misfirings cause vertigo: sensations of extreme dizziness, nausea, and confusion that make people think they are falling when they are on solid ground. Motion sickness—car sickness, seasickness, airsickness—also can be caused when the body's motion sensors fail to catch up with rapid changes in position.

A similar but opposite problem occurs to some people when they work with virtual reality. In VR, users' bodies generally stay in one place even though they see their perspectives change as they move through a virtual environment. VR users move their heads and arms as they interact with the environment, but they do not experience the proprioceptive cues that would accompany moving their bodies across space. The discrepancy between what a VR user sees and what he or she feels can create symptoms similar to those of motion sickness. Called *simulator sickness, cyberspace sickness,* or simply *cybersickness,* the feelings of nausea and disorientation can limit how long some people can work with HMD-based VR systems and even some shutter-glass displays.

Simulator sickness is not unique to immersive computing experiences. The malady can strike pilots who train in flight simulators, even those mounted on motion platforms. No matter how rapidly these moving simulators respond to a pilot's actions or how far they tilt, they cannot duplicate the effects of upside-down flight or all the forces of acceleration present in the real world. The physical sensations do not match up exactly to what pilots see during their training session, leading to the same types of motion sickness that people can experience on board ships, in cars, or on airplanes.

Successfully adjusting to the limitations of flight simulators can lead to other problems that are related to simulator sickness, however. Over the course of a training session, the brain begins to accept the absence of certain sensations—the acceleration pilots feel as their jets climb into the air, the pressure they feel as they make a tight midair turn—as normal. If a pilot takes to the air too soon after a simulator session, the return of these sensations can throw his or her perceptions into a brief period of confusion—enough, in some cases, for the pilot to lose control of the plane.

VR researchers expected to encounter these types of problems. "We always knew that we had a potential problem with simulator sickness," said Tom Furness, who learned of the phenomenon during his days as a researcher for the U.S. Air Force. "Even from the early days of flight simulators, we knew that. Pilots were not allowed to fly the real airplane until they had been away from the simulator at least twenty-four hours, because there was this problem . . . where you're rolling the aircraft in the simulator but you're not really rolling the body. So this disconnect would require some reorientation."

Decompressing from VR

The level of simulator sickness that affects VR users is not quite as severe as the level that simulator-trained pilots go through. But VR users have had to deal with other forms of disorientation after working in virtual environments for a long time. Users see reality as somewhat "unreal" after focusing on a computer's monitor screen for hours at an end. This sensation can last from a couple of minutes to more than half an hour, depending on the individual and how long she or he has been working.

People who work with regular, nonimmersive desktop computers can have trouble with this effect as well, because people perceive computer-graphics environments and reality differently. The images we see of reality are regular; shadows blend smoothly with the edges of objects, small items can easily be separated from one another, and objects at medium-to-long distances can be noticed if not identified. Computer graphics, on the other hand, are made up of sharp edges and lines. Even when created by advanced graphics supercomputers, objects that seem smooth and round are made up of angled polygons and combinations of differently shaded color blocks called *pixels*. Computer-graphics artists use a range of programming techniques to smooth out the rough edges and create the illusion of curved surfaces. Even so, the eyes and brain have to work harder to perceive and translate the computer images as something approaching reality.

The type of display a system uses also makes a difference. Even though it is barely noticeable, cathode-ray tubes constantly flicker as their electron beams scan over the face of the display screen. People usually do not notice this flickering, but its presence does strain the user's eyes. Liquid-crystal displays do not have the flicker problem of CRTs, but they do not have the tight picture definition of a typical CRT, either. Instead, LCD screens form images by combining hundreds or thousands of pixels into patterns that the brain blurs into a coherent image. In older HMDs that used liquid-crystal displays, the screens were so close to the eyes that users focused as much on the individual blocks of color as on the images those blocks created. Users often had to squint to blur the pixels into a recognizable image; this caused headaches. Fortunately, modern LCDs have smaller pixels and much better levels of resolution, reducing much of this strain.

Then there are the psychological problems that crop up when people spend a long time working in VR. Because the immersive VR experience comes mostly from visual and audio simulation, only the visual and audio processing areas of the brain receive any real stimulation. But our brains are set up to process the physical as well as the audio and visual signals associated with moving through the physical world. Since VR only presents audio and visual cues, the brain has to mimic its own physical cues. When the brain fails to do this, the user can develop the symptoms of motion sickness, as described earlier. When the brain succeeds in fooling itself, though, it sometimes cannot stop even when the VR session is over. Just as a pilot's brain can rewire itself in a flight simulator, a VR user's brain can become accustomed to accepting virtual environment input as "real." This phenomenon can lead to such problems as "virtual flashbacks," in which people suddenly feel that they no longer are in a physical environment.

Unfortunately, these types of physical problems are just par for the course of virtual reality. People have to decide if their desire to work with virtual environments outweighs the discomfort that some virtual-environment effectors cause. Future developments probably will eliminate many of these problems, and a few manufacturers have incorporated some solutions into their products. Some head-mounted displays, for example, have their screens on a hinge. VR users thus can lift the screens out of the way for a short "reality break" from their virtual environments.

Researchers also have discovered that using a few simple virtual-environment programming techniques can prevent these problems from developing in the first place. These techniques include placing graphical cues in the environments that serve as visual anchors for the brain. By including an unmoving object or image in the environment— as part of the background, for example—and making sure the user can see it wherever he or she moves, environment designers can balance out the discrepancy between what the user sees and what he or she feels.

Decompressing from virtual environments can be tricky, because the reprogramming is not simply a temporary or a long-term effect.

"It actually is both temporary and long-term," Furness said. "We've noticed you can re-adapt to the real world quickly, but you still retain the coefficients [the relationships the brain forms between the appearance of movement and the body's lack of movement] that you stored for running your virtual-world environments. When you're now filling your visual world, then you can cause problems with it. So we need to proceed very carefully and systematically in understanding the human factors side of this."

The Human Factor

As if the problems within the VR user's heads were not bad enough, VR tools can have negative effects on the rest of the body as well. Even though virtual reality is a computing technology, it is a computing technology that involves strapping equipment onto the human body. Many virtual-reality systems require their users to wear some sort of apparatus. One of the most commonly used pieces of VR body wear is the head-mounted display. Compared to the Sword of Damocles, which had to be supported by a metal post, modern HMDs are very light. Some full-size HMDs weigh as little as four and a half pounds, while shutter glasses, LCD-screen glasses, and visor-style displays weigh even less.

Unfortunately, this weight is placed on top of the head and spinal column, a structure that can be thought of as a bowling ball on top of a pipe cleaner. HMD manufacturers do their best to ensure that the weight of their displays is evenly balanced, but the muscles and the vertebrae of the neck still must adjust themselves to support and control this extra weight. Shutter glasses require their users to hold their heads fairly straight and steady as they work with their virtual environments to maintain the 3-D illusion. Even with visor displays, users can move their heads only as far as the interface cord connecting them to the computer allows. The added strain on the head and neck muscles can cause severe headaches and muscle aches, especially after long VR sessions.

Physical differences between users also can make it difficult to find effectors that fit. A head-mounted display, a pair of shutter glasses, or a wired glove that works well for some people will be too big or too small for others. Even the difference between people's eyes can affect the success of an immersive experience. In most people, the distance between the pupils ranges from two to three inches. Because stereoscopic vision involves mixing two slightly different images of the same scene, VR systems have to have some way to adjust for these differences in pupil distance.

Manufacturers have had to design VR tools that can accommodate all the different head sizes, hand sizes, and even levels of dexterity among potential users. Just as clothing manufacturers have done, some VR companies design products that come in a fixed range of sizes that fit most of the people who need to use them. Others build equipment that can be adjusted to fit each person who uses it. Consider the problem of creating stereoscopic vision displays. Systems that use shutter glasses, polarized lenses, or other methods to turn monitors into three-dimensional displays address the issue automatically: The lenses usually are big enough for everyone who uses them (though the frames can be uncomfortable for some people). In helmet- and visor-style HMDs and for LCD eyeglass-style displays, the screen size is limited. Some manufacturers have worked around this problem by making the screens themselves adjustable, with knobs that move the screens toward or away from the user's nose until they reach the correct distance. In other models, the screens are far enough from the face for most users' eyes to adjust with little difficulty.

Of course, virtual reality is not unique in presenting problems for users. People who use computers—as well as people in noncomputer fields, such as meat cutters and dentists—have long risked developing injuries such as carpal tunnel syndrome, a swelling of one of the nerves that runs through the wrist to fingers. One of the things that cause carpal tunnel syndrome is performing the same hand and wrist motions over and over again, including typing on keyboards or using computer mice that are positioned at an awkward angle. Other types of injuries—including muscle strains, tendon inflammation, and numbness in the fingers—also can result from repeatedly doing the same task. These maladies generally are referred to as repetitive-motion or repetitive-strain injuries.

All forms of computer technology, from office computers to home video-game consoles, carry these risks. In fact, late in January 2001, a group of British doctors announced that using vibrating video-game controllers could cause hand and arm problems similar to those seen in workers who use heavy industrial tools. The controllers were of a type designed to provide a limited sense of tactile feedback. However, the doctors, who practiced in a children's hospital, reported that one of their patients had developed problems after using the controllers for nearly seven hours a day—far more time than a lot of people would spend playing games and enough time for the cumulative effect of the vibrations to weaken the patient's hand muscles. It is easy to imagine how similar problems could develop in people who use VR tools for an extended time.

20

VIRTUAL PHILOSOPHY

Virtual reality's pioneers and supporters believe that immersive computing could become a powerful tool for expanding knowledge, creativity, and insight into the world. But virtual reality has turned out to be more than just a new method for interacting with computers. Its creation, together with the development of other advanced computing techniques, also brought about a whole new way of thinking about how people can interact with their computers. Because working within digital environments that are designed to mimic the physical world is far different from standard methods for handling computer data, the creation of VR has posed some serious philosophical questions about the use of advanced technology that still have to be answered.

For some researchers, the big questions revolve around whether or not VR ultimately will benefit or harm its users. Just because a technology like virtual reality can be built, does that mean it should be built? How far should VR systems go in replicating the sensations of the real world, and at what point might those systems go too far? Digital environment technology can be a great help to the people who use it for serious work or as a creative outlet, but it also could pose significant problems if people become dependent on it as a means of escaping the real world or use it to avoid dealing with other people face-to-face.

There are less weighty problems to consider as well. Some involve questions about the technology itself, such as whether or not an experience needs to be fully immersive in order to be considered "virtual reality." Some people, for example, have proclaimed that a text-only interface can be considered a form of virtual reality if it connects users to a sufficiently detailed text-based environment. The argument in favor of this idea is that, like graphical VR, text systems allow people to put themselves in fully contained environments, only ones of words and imagination, not tools and graphics. The opposite viewpoint, of course, is that a digital environment is "virtual" only if it includes a three-dimensional graphic space and provides a way for users to navigate through the computer-generated realm.

Answering the questions about what qualifies a digital environment as virtual reality can help researchers and companies refine and expand VR technology, but why are questions about the ultimate benefit or harm of VR important? One reason is that these questions can help minimize the hazards of using high-tech devices such as VR. For all their enthusiasm, researchers and supporters see VR as a tool full of dangers as well as possibilities—dangers that come not just from the physical drawbacks of VR, but from possible psychological responses from VR users. Some VR developers even fear that devising tools and environments that provide realistic experiences might end up stifling the creative response and interaction that computer pioneers had been striving to bring about. Debating whether VR is becoming a tool that enhances or impairs human activity can provide guidelines for building future generations of virtual environments.

Is VR Following the Right Path?

When a reporter asked the explorer George Mallory, who was one of the first men to attempt climbing Mount Everest, why he wanted to, he replied, "Because it is there." A similar spirit drives many of those who get involved in virtual-reality work—the fact that the VR exists and the lure of what people might be able to do with it entices men and women to adopt or improve on the technology. In fact, the development of virtual reality itself, with all of its setbacks and limitations, can be seen as a journey across a range of mountains, a journey in which reaching the top of one peak reveals the presence of an even larger one on the other side. But many people who have taken part in this journey, as well as some outside the field, wonder if the path they are on is one they should be following.

Part of the popularity of immersive computing research comes from the idea that computers can be machines that help people think, which inspired scientists like Ivan Sutherland and Douglas Engelbart to begin making computers "user-friendly" in the 1950s and 1960s. Remember, one of Engelbart's illustrations for his view of future computer technology was for an interactive architectural "drawing table" that took over most, if not all, of the engineering and mathematical tasks, giving the architect more time to concentrate on a home's design. Such systems have been available for years in two-dimensional and nonimmersive three-dimensional programs, and many architectural firms use 3-D animation techniques to create and display views of proposed buildings. Immersive systems, as discussed earlier, can make this process even better, allowing people to walk through buildings and find areas for improvement before construction begins.

Similar enhancements in other fields show that VR truly can become a tool for boosting the human intellect, unleashing creativity and freeing people from having to handle routine tasks that computers can perform more quickly. That has been the ideal of computer technology in general, not simply of virtual reality. But ideals rarely last long once people begin using new technologies. When the first modern televisions were produced in the 1930s, they were thought of much as VR is thought of today. Some people saw them as nothing more than expensive toys; others saw them as potential windows to the world that would lead to a golden age of information. Television had the potential to become a tool that would educate and inform viewers, as well as entertain them, and that would increase understanding between people as it brought the world closer together. (A historic broadcast in the 1950s emphasized the ability of television to shrink distances, when journalist Edward R. Murrow brought images of the Atlantic and Pacific Coasts of the United States into his audience's living rooms at the same time, something that had never been done before.)

In television's early years, shows that featured educational topics, government affairs, and cultural events were fixtures of each week's programming schedule. As worthwhile as these shows were, however, they did not draw as many viewers as comedies, soap operas, sports shows, and other popular programs. Television stations and networks make money based on how many viewers they can attract. The possibly more important but definitely less profitable shows moved to times when fewer people in general watched television, were taken over by public television stations, or went off the air altogether. These days, critics decry the number of daytime talk programs, infomercials, and exploitive reality-based shows that have become staples of modern television. And when health experts warn of the dangers of leading an inactive life, they most often refer to people who watch television for hours on end.

Other products of modern progress have had similar unforeseen side effects. Automobiles gave people the ability to travel long distances quickly, yet tens of thousands of people die in car accidents every year. Telephones are convenient communication tools, but more and more people are finding their dinnertimes interrupted by unwanted and annoying telemarketing calls. Virtual reality still is too new a technology and has not been widely used enough for these types of side effects to be revealed. We still do not know if having computer simulations of the physical world or computer environments that are not possible in the physical world ultimately will be good or harmful.

Some researchers also worry that their tools for enhancing the human intellect could turn into substitutes for human creativity. Instead of using VR to spark their imaginations and test out new ideas for use in the real world, people might use virtual environments to shut themselves off from reality or to copy the work of already-proven designs like a word processor can copy chapters from a book. If people spend enough time working and playing in virtual reality, they might not want to bother dealing with the real world. And the fact that the virtual environments they work and play in can be changed and reset might cause users to overlook the fact that actions in the physical world have long-lasting consequences.

With possible outcomes such as these, as well as the physiological drawbacks to VR, the issue becomes less a matter of whether various tools and environments *can* be developed or more a matter of whether they *should* be developed. As HIT Lab director Tom Furness puts it, "Are we doing the right thing? Are we climbing the right mountain? Yeah, we can build this incredibly powerful, engaging environment, this virtual medium, but what good is going to come out of it?" These and similar questions may be answered in years to come.

What *Really* Is Virtual Reality?

Even though "virtual reality" is just one of the terms given to the technology of immersive computing, it became the most widely used of these terms partly because it summed up what the technology was all about. Virtual reality indeed offered sensations that, at first, seemed virtually the same as those of real life, and it provided interactions with digital environments that were virtually identical to the way people work in the real world. The word *virtual* also was applied to the worlds that VR created ("virtual worlds," "virtual environments," "virtual spaces"); the objects within those worlds ("virtual buildings," "virtual furniture"); and even the experiences the environments mimicked ("virtual medicine," "virtual architecture").

Before long, the news media and the general public began applying the word *virtual* to anything that could be done with computers, whether in the form of an immersive environment or not. Exchanging messages using dial-up bulletin boards or within chat rooms became "virtual communication." People formed "virtual communities" of discussion groups, sharing information on topics of mutual interest over data lines. Later in the 1990s, real-estate agents began offering "virtual tours" of homes by placing two-dimensional floor plans and photographs of each room of the house on their companies' Web pages. The term *virtual medicine* started referring to information available on medical websites as well as to experimental surgical simulators, while the term *virtual training* was attached to some training systems that incorporated two-dimensional computer graphics into their schedules.

The virtually unlimited application of the word *virtual* to mean "computerized" began conflicting with the idea of immersive computing as being something different from standard computing. Was VR really a new, unique area of technology, or was it just an extension of standard computing? Even the people who worked in the field had different views of what the term *virtual reality* represented. For those outside the field, the issue of what virtual reality was and what it was not was simply confusing.

Video games helped blur the boundary lines that separated VR from other forms of computing. Most video games—whether cabinet-size arcade machines, home video-gaming systems, or computers that have been set up as game machines—use two-dimensional monitors or television sets. The programs these machines run, though, have become extremely sophisticated over the past decade, with lifelike characters moving through richly detailed environments that require game players to navigate in three directions. Arcade games that have force-feedback controls or on motion platforms to make the experience even more realistic are as close as many people will come to virtual reality. For many people, this level of interaction is enough to be considered the equivalent of a VR experience.

Answers to the question of what makes virtual reality a separate technology still vary from person to person, but there are some principles that separate VR from other types of computing. The fact that a gaming or working environment is three-dimensional does not necessarily qualify it as a virtual experience. The key element to virtual reality is the sense of immersion it creates and the feeling that the digital environment is similar to a user's real-world experiences. In general, this means providing stereoscopic vision, a means of moving throughout the environment (preferably in three dimensions), and some way to interact with digital objects in an easily understood manner.

Then comes the question of how immersive an experience has to be for it to be virtual reality. Over the years, some computer users have held on to the idea that text-only environments can be considered virtual reality. Many computer adventure games in the 1970s and 1980s, in fact, were based on text descriptions of underground kingdoms or outer-space adventures, with players typing in commands to move around or interact with characters within the game. So-called text-based VR combined the level of description and interaction of types of games with the real-time interaction of on-line chat rooms. Because computers kept track of which objects were in which rooms, some people felt that these nongraphic digital environments fulfilled the goals of VR.

In general, though, "real" virtual reality is based on visual computing and a form of interaction not tied to computer keyboards. A three-dimensional environment displayed on a two-dimensional screen—with shutter glasses to provide a sense of depth, 3-D joysticks, or force-feedback effectors for maneuvering, and three-dimensional sound—can meet many people's expectations for a virtual-reality experience. But VRML-style Web browsers, which use three-dimensional environments to display data, do not include stereoscopic effects. Like 3-D computer games, their displays use shading, diminishing perspective, and other techniques to create the impression of a physical environment on a two-dimensional monitor screen. Computer users can navigate and interact with these environments using mouse and keyboard commands, but the effect is much like playing a 3-D computer game. For many people who take part in on-line, graphically oriented communities, though, this level of interaction is just fine.

Another type of Web-based environment, called panoramic virtual reality, presents 360-degree photographs of real-world locations, such as forests or city plazas, similar to what a person would see by standing in one place and turning all the way around. A creation of Apple Computer Inc. called QuickTime VR uses a series of photographs to create a long panorama of a location in the real world. The photographs are made using a camera mounted on a pivot to capture the scene as it might look to someone turning in a complete circle. The photos then are scanned into a computer and graphically stitched together. When the work is done, the entire circular view is spread across the computer screen like an unrolled label from a can of soup. The portion in the center of the screen represents the view in front of the user; the left and right sides of the display show equal portions of the rear view. Users can "turn around" or change to different viewpoints using a standard 2-D computer mouse.

Panoramic VR displays also can provide an illusion of movements, allowing users to zoom in on and away from areas of the photograph and giving them the opportunity to click on links to other panoramic photos or to information files. However, there is even less of a connection to "true" virtual reality than is present in a VRML browser's window. Because these images are two dimensional, they do not offer the sense of depth and immersion found in other displays. Thus, many people involved in virtual reality do not consider these panoramic environments to be "real" VR. Even though users can zoom in on and away from areas of the photograph, there is no way to interact with the display, aside from clicking on links to information files or other photographs. Again, different people have different opinions on whether or not such displays are useful. Just as millions of computer users are satisfied with desktop PCs instead of multimillion-dollar supercomputers, many users are satisfied with these panoramic displays.

Virtual Reality's Image

Then there is the issue of virtual reality's image. VR has been praised and scoffed at—usually at the same time—ever since it was created. Depending on their outlook, people have called VR a tool that would allow humanity to achieve a new level of knowledge and insight, as well as a gimmick that was good for playing video games but not for serious computing.

The hyperbole surrounding VR in the 1990s and the widespread use of "virtual" for almost any type of computer activity made it difficult to sustain serious public interest in the technology. (The expense of VR systems and the limits to what they could do did not help matters, either.) Even today, many researchers are reluctant to use the term *virtual reality* when talking about their work. Instead, they refer to it as immersive computing, virtual-environment technology, or some other term that has the same meaning without raising embarrassing images.

On the other hand, "virtual reality" still is a clear, effective way to identify this style of computing and is a term with which most people are familiar. Reporters and writers can use the term without having to explain what it means. For companies that sell the hardware and software of immersive computing, "virtual reality" provides an easy handle for their marketing efforts. And in recent years, news stories have featured successful applications of VR technology, such as its use as a psychological therapy tool or as a means to distract patients during painful medical procedures, in a straightforward manner, without raising the specter of hype.

Researchers hope that future improvements to and a more widespread use of virtual reality will overcome its gimmicky reputation, much as personal computers overcame the image of computing as a feat limited to governments, universities, and big corporations. But these future developments also will have to overcome another image— the one presented in science-fiction stories, movies, and television shows. In fact, the idea of placing characters inside computer-generated worlds appeared in fiction long before virtual reality existed. While they did not appear as often as faster-than-light spaceships or high-energy ray guns, computer-controlled displays that simulated distant lands or projected digitized information directly into the mind of a story's hero popped up in stories about the dangers of using technology that came too close to reproducing reality. These stories date back to the middle of the last century—"The Veldt" by Ray Bradbury, the story mentioned in chapter 5 in which one room of a house displayed a segment of the African plains, appeared in the early 1950s. Three decades later, the novel *Neuromancer* by William Gibson introduced the concept of "cyberspace," a three-dimensional visual representation of all the world's linked computer networks, in which legitimate workers and digital criminals alike worked with computer data. Many other writers had their own methods for blending human perception with computer data.

Shortly after virtual reality appeared in newspaper headlines, it started showing up as a plot device in movies such as *Lawnmower Man*, a film about a scientist who increases the intelligence of a gardener using VR, and television shows such as "VR5," in which a telephone service technician and computer hobbyist discovers how to enter other people's minds through the phone system. In designing visually pleasing representations of the technology, special-effects technicians were able to let their imaginations run free. Big-budget films in particular presented visions of VR that had been created using the most advanced computer-animation tools available at the time. Audiences saw representations of digital environments that were far more advanced than anything real VR systems could accomplish, in which the movie's characters seemed to merge completely with virtual worlds. The fact that these shows and movies often used real-life VR tools as props helped heighten the effect.

True, there is little risk of people confusing the fantasy images of VR with the real technology, just as there is little risk of confusing special-effects representations of space travel with what happens during real space flights. VR tools are not yet able to make people forget they are working in a digital environment rather than the real world, and most environments are not yet as nicely rendered as those in the movies. Nor are the fantasy images of VR harmful in themselves—VR researchers have mentioned science-fiction representations to illustrate the goals of their work. One image in particular has been used many times: the Holodeck of the *Star Trek* television series, which displays any object or environment a starship crewman desired. Even so, the tidy presentations of VR that have been used as tools of storytelling still will pose a challenge to how the public accepts the real thing, once it becomes available.

VR'S FUTURE

Virtual reality's quirky history, with its technological setbacks and drawbacks, often has raised doubts that this type of computing would have much of a future at all. Some computer specialists and other experts have called VR little more than a toy that would have few, if any, lasting effects. Less skeptical experts believe that VR will have a useful place in computing but that, as happened with computers in general, it would be decades before the technology improves to the point where people can use it in everyday applications. The true outcome of all the work that has been done in the field of VR remains to be seen.

Even so, the advances made since VR's invention indicate that it will have a strong future. Men and women who work in the field of immersive computing may feel uneasy about using the term *virtual reality*, but the fact is that the technology and goals of virtual reality have been a steady, though small, presence in the computer industry for more than 10 years. Using computer interfaces that allow people to work the way they do in real life still is seen as a better method than requiring people to stare at flat video screens and type on keyboards. VR continues to offer a good alternative to standard computer displays for tasks such as data visualization for science, engineering, architecture, and other professions. And the tools of VR have been adapted to other uses, giving more evidence that the technology is here to stay.

This does not mean that virtual reality's time has arrived, or even that it is about to have a major breakout. As mentioned in chapter 1, Dr. Frederick Brooks, one of the pioneers in the computing field that became virtual reality, wrote in 2000 that VR took a decade to go from being a technology that "almost works" to being a technology that "barely works." The tools of VR and the environments available to VR users, Brooks and other researchers have said, still have not reached the point of offering the ideal, seamless connection between people and data that is required. While an individual haptic manipulator, HMD, or tracking device may perform its task well, the field of immersive computing as a whole has a long way to go.

Thawing VR's Winter

At the turn of the 21st century, many of the obstacles facing VR's development were the same as those that plagued the technology in the past: computing power, accurate tracking, digital environment design, and, of course, high costs. Computers today, including desktop PCs, are far more powerful than they were even in the late 1990s, and they can serve as the engines for remarkably advanced digital environments. Still, the most useful immersive computing experiences are those that are powered by the most advanced computers, such as high-end supercomputers that share tasks among many linked processors. Coordinating the movements of a user's head and hands with the digital-environment display still takes a lot of effort: trackers have to be wired up and calibrated, and users have to adjust themselves to the added weight and wiring of their effectors. Because there are no software tools that allow designers to build three-dimensional worlds within an immersive design environment, this work takes place mostly on two-dimensional computer screens. And the most successful VR systems still are the ones that are the most expensive, up to $1 million for displays such as the CAVE.

These obstacles have made their presence felt ever since the 1980s and are a large part of the reason why VR has had trouble breaking out of its "winter" period. Overcoming these obstacles will take years of research and large amounts of money. Despite many interesting experimental and real-world applications of VR technology, there have been no truly ground-breaking developments—no "killer apps" like business spreadsheets for microcomputers or e-mail for Internet users—to create widespread demand for VR. Though new technologies may be neat, the companies that produce those technologies need to make a profit; fewer companies are able or willing to build products that appeal to a limited number of customers, unless those customers can provide a high enough level of business.

However, companies are willing to spend money to develop products that might appeal to a vast number of potential customers. Throughout the 1990s, consumer electronics firms have incorporated elements of virtual reality in products not designed strictly for VR systems. Force-feedback joystick and steering wheel game controllers are examples of this jump from immersive computing laboratories to electronics stores' shelves. The fact that companies keep developing these products for non-VR uses and, more importantly, that people have bought them shows there is at least some desire for such tools among the general public. For this reason, and because enough applications of true virtual reality have shown that the technology is useful, corporations are willing to conduct or support research into improving the technology.

So, where is the future of immersive computing being developed? Some of the work takes place in corporate workshops; a lot more takes place in university laboratories and research centers, many of which form business partnerships with companies and government agencies outside the academic world. The HIT Lab at the University of Washington, mentioned elsewhere in this book, is one example of this type of immersive computing incubator. Another is the Integrated Media Systems Center (IMSC) at the University of Southern California in Los Angeles, one of a number of VR-related research groups the university operates. There, research projects are tools for hands-on learning as much as they are vehicles for advancing the state of the art. For all the cutting-edge work that goes on there, however, the center's laboratories at first look much like any other office, with people working quietly on computer equipment spread out on shelves and desktops. Then the visitor starts noticing small details, such as a large grid attached to a section of a room's ceiling that serves as part of a motion-tracking system or a set of shutter glasses left sitting next to a keyboard. Another room is set up as a miniature theater, complete with a wide display screen and another type of motion-tracking system, for presentations of the center's latest developments. Even the offices of the center's faculty and staff contain reminders of the work being done, from computing equipment to framed articles featuring some of the center's recent projects.

Around the world, research groups such as the IMSC continue the drive to make immersive computing possible. "Various things we do fall along the spectrum from 'ready for lab or commercial use' all the way to the fairly far out, where we know how to do something, but we don't quite know what it's good for yet, or we don't know what form it might make sense to put that in, as far as developing a product" says Dr. Ulrich Neumann, the center's director and one of its researchers.

Much of the work at the center, Neumann says, involves questions of basic science and technology, where researchers have to invent solutions to problems and questions that no one else has ever had to deal with before. Occasionally, a company or another researcher will learn of the solution and want the centers to develop it into a useable, marketable form. "That's exciting, and we like it when those things happen, but our primary role is not as businesspeople," Neumann says. "So we have to have some other person or entity to help us make the transition from technology sitting in a lab to something that's a real product."

Because research facilities are designed to invent, rather than exploit, new technologies, universities establish such groups as the IMSC to ease the transition from the laboratory to the marketplace. And because maintaining or expanding research and development departments is expensive, businesses often are happy to pay the comparatively lower cost of supporting university projects in exchange for the right to develop the results into products. As a result, future virtual-environment applications are likely to come from these academic partnerships as from laboratory or corporate research work alone.

The Best of Both Worlds?

Over the years, virtual reality has proven to be a useful engineering tool that allows companies to cut the amount of real-world work that has to be done. Many companies have saved millions of dollars designing virtual prototypes for the machines they make. Likewise, augmented reality, the technology that overlays three-dimensional graphics onto the physical world, promises to be as useful a tool for building these machines as VR is for designing them.

The aerospace industry has been one of the leading institutions in the drive to perfect augmented reality as an everyday tool. A typical commercial airplane has thousands of miles worth of wires, cables, fuel lines, and hydraulic lines that have to be installed just right. In addition, the body and wings of an airplane are a complex system of girders, metal sheets, and connectors that all have to line up correctly. One of the trickiest tasks in assembling an airplane is correctly reading the blueprints that refer to its millions of separate parts. And an equally tricky task in maintaining an airplane is correctly reading the manuals that refer to its intricately linked electrical, mechanical, and hydraulic systems.

Augmented-reality assembly or maintenance rigs could help workers eliminate the need to switch their attention from their work to their blueprints and back again. A computer-generated representation of a system's assembly instructions would be projected on a monocle or a pair of work goggles over the system being assembled. By matching a few key points on the work surface with similar points in the instructions, the computer controlling the display would ensure that both the display and the physical objects lined up—for example, pointing out where workers needs to drill holes in parts that need to be attached to one another.

This is the goal of a number of programs being conducted around the world—by or with the assistance of major airplane manufacturers—to develop AR systems that can point out where workers need to drill holes in airplane parts or project aircraft maintenance instructions. Researchers also have experimented with easing less-intricate tasks with augmented reality, such as solving the mysteries of photocopier repair by merging maintenance instructions with the technician's view of the machine. Other inventors have been developing a range of wearable computers that might aid people in their daily lives: displaying a map directing visitors to museums or hotels; enhancing the office of a clerical worker with virtual phone directories and message boards; or presenting architectural or structural data about various buildings to building inspectors or superintendents.

The trick with developing these systems has been getting computers to place digital images exactly where they need to be on a user's HMD or eyepiece and to adjust the image as the user moves around. So far, demonstration models of AR systems have come very close to providing the necessary levels of accuracy and speed, but few have come close enough to the desired level of reliability. Moreover, while researchers have built many experimental wearable AR systems, these have tended to be heavy and awkward to wear, often incorporating laptop computers and tracking devices mounted on metal backpack frames. The hope is that as computer technology improves and as researchers gain more experience in teaching computers how to overlap the real and virtual worlds, AR systems will become practical enough for everyday use.

Closing In on the "Ultimate Display"

It has been more than four decades since computer scientists began developing their dreams for creating digitized realms of computer data. Researchers have made many remarkable advances in computing technology during this time and have encountered many remarkable false starts and dead ends as well. But they continue to work toward their goal of developing computers that provide a more convenient form of interaction than is available today. Even so, it will take a lot of effort to perfect the immersive computer technology that has been created so far, much less to bring about an era of truly invisible, transparent computing.

Still, people continue to find hope for such a future in work that is being done today. Some envision a time when the Internet provides a high enough level of data transmission to enable real-time VR interaction from home computers, offices, and schoolrooms. Others are working on teleconferencing systems that use multiple video cameras, head trackers, and other VR tools to erase the distance between colleagues in different offices, creating the illusion that someone in another city is sitting at the next desk over. Among the people involved with research into the creation of these virtual-reality meeting places is the man who gave virtual reality its most well-recognized name—Jaron Lanier, whose work with a group called the National Tele-Immersion Initiative already has created a number of promising demonstrations of this new form of virtual-reality networking.

Elsewhere, scientists and engineers continue to improve the effectors that provide the physical cues of virtual reality. Graphics displays, from HMDs to stereoscopic computer screens, are gaining higher levels of resolution. Haptic manipulators are providing progressively more accurate sensation of texture and solidity. Some researchers are exploring methods of incorporating the sense of smell into computing, using fans that blow odors—such as the scent of flowers or well-aged wine—from scent cartridges to the user's nose.

There even has been a step or two taken toward the goal of giving computers control over matter. Virtual prototyping, in which engineers create and test parts and equipment in a three-dimensional computer display, now has a physical counterpart—three-dimensional, rapid prototyping, in which computer-controlled machines create physical models of digital designs. Some of these model-making machines are similar to industrial robots, using drills and other tools to carve objects from solid blocks of material. Others use lasers to congeal liquid resins, building objects layer by layer. Though not virtual reality in and of themselves, these devices are another step on the path to giving computer data a more realistic appearance.

A Final Note

There is a rule of thumb in computer science, called Moore's law, that computers double in power about every two years. That is, each new generation of computers work twice as fast, can handle twice as many functions at one time, and in general are twice as good as those available two years before. (Gordon Moore, one of the cofounders of computer chip maker Intel Corporation, first made this observation during the 1960s.) Virtual reality, which is a combination of computers, hardware, and special software, seems to be following a slower but steadier path of development. But as with all other technologies, virtual reality's path can always change, speeding up if researchers suddenly make a series of breakthroughs or slowing down if interest in a particular application wanes.

This book reflects the status of virtual reality as it was toward the end of 2001. The technology of virtual reality undoubtedly has changed since then. HMDs may have improved, or computers may have developed to the point where lag times in rendering virtual environments are irrelevant. One of the best places to find out the most recent developments in VR is on the Internet, which itself seems to have a strong future. Searching the World Wide Web under the categories of "virtual reality," "virtual environments," "immersive computing," or any of the other terms used in this book should yield enough information to satisfy anyone's curiosity. Otherwise, scanning newspaper and magazine listings such as *The Reader's Guide to Periodic Literature* or computerized sources should point the way to the most up-to-date information.

GLOSSARY

3DOF   *See* THREE-DEGREE-OF-FREEDOM.

6DOF   *See* SIX-DEGREE-OF-FREEDOM.

amplitude   A measure of the amount of disturbance created by a wave. The amplitude of a wave on a lake, for example, is the distance between the top (crest) or bottom (trough) of the wave and the surface of the lake when it is calm.

application   A computer program that enables a user to do a specific task. Word processors and games are types of applications.

artificial reality   A computer display controlled by the interaction of the user's image with the displayed environment. Computer scientist and artist Myron Krueger coined this term.

augmented reality   A computer display that seems to overlay computer-generated images onto real-world objects. Usually, this effect involves projecting the computer images onto a head-mounted display, a special pair of glasses, or a small monitor that hangs in front of one eye.

autostereoscopic   A computer display that can create the illusion of 3-D sight without requiring the user to wear special glasses or other equipment.

axis   A mathematical term that refers to the three directions of movement in the physical world. The plural of axis is axes (pronounced "acks-eez"). The three axes are the X (left/right) axis; the Y (up/down) axis; and the Z (forward/back) axis. These three axes also are known as the Cartesian axes.

binocular parallax   The brain's ability to perceive three-dimensional depth and distance by combining the slightly offset images sensed by each eye.

cathode-ray tube (CRT)   A vacuum tube that forms images by shooting electrons from a negatively charged source (a cathode) to a phosphorescent screen that glows when hit by the electrons. Electromagnets inside the vacuum tube bend the beam, forcing it to rapidly scan across the surface of the screen. Color television sets and computer monitors have differently colored screens in the same CRT.

CD-ROM   *See* COMPACT DISK—READ ONLY MEMORY.

circuit   A pathway for electricity formed by the wires in an electrical device.

circuit board   A board in a computer or other electronic device that houses microprocessors or other components connected by printed or etched wire circuits.

compact disk (CD)   A plastic-covered aluminum disk that contains digital information in the form of small pits etched into the disk's surface by a laser. CDs can be used to store either computer data or sound tracks. (CDs were created as a smaller alternative to 12-to-14-inch optical disks.)

compact disk—read only memory (CD-ROM)   A compact disk that contains text, audio, and visual computer files, which can be read by a computer drive but which cannot be altered.

computer graphics   Visual displays created using computers. Technically, a simple bar graph created with a word processor is an example of computer graphics. However, the term usually refers to more advanced displays such as those in video games or flight simulators.

CRT   *See* CATHODE-RAY TUBE.

cyberspace   The imagined world created by the Internet and other computer networks in which people communicate and share information. William Gibson, a science-fiction author, created the word in his 1983 novel *Neuromancer.*

database   A collection of information stored as a computer file that is set up to allow people to easily retrieve that information.

desktop computer   In general, any computer that can fit on top of a desk. *See* PERSONAL COMPUTER.

diorama   A physical display that re-creates a scene from nature, history, or literature.

effector   Any device used to display or control a virtual environment.

electric potential   The ease with which any material conducts electricity. Electric potential is measured in volts.

electromagnetic force   In physics, the combined properties of electricity and magnetism. Electricity and magnetism are very similar forces: Every electric current generates a magnetic field, and every magnetic field can be made to generate an electric current. Because electricity and magnetism are so strongly linked, scientists consider them to be aspects of the same force. Other examples of electromagnetic force are light waves, radio waves, and microwave radiation.

fiber optics   The use of optical fibers to transmit information.

flight simulator   A device or computer program that reproduces the effects of airplane or helicopter flight.

force ball   A stationary, ball-shaped effector that reacts to pushing and twisting forces applied to the ball by the user, letting the user navigate virtual environments.

force-feedback   An effector that mimics weight, solidity, or other physical sensations through motorized resistance to a user's movements.

frequency   A measurement of how many waves travel through a substance in a given amount of time. For example, humans can hear from as few as 15 to as many as 20,000 sound waves per second.

graphics board   A microprocessor circuit board that is designed specifically to calculate and render computer graphics.

gyroscope   A device that uses a rapidly spinning mass mounted in a freely moving framework to maintain its orientation.

gyroscopic tracker   A position tracker that uses gyroscopes to detect which way a VR user moves.

haptic   Related to the sense of touch.

head-mounted display (HMD)   A computer or television monitor that rests on or otherwise attaches to the head of a user. HMDs can incorporate headphones and position trackers and can provide either a semitransparent view (as in augmented reality) or a fully enclosed display (as with most VR systems).

HMD   *See* HEAD-MOUNTED DISPLAY.

hype   Short for hyperbole; overexaggerated accounts of how good or bad an object or an event is.

hypertext   A computer programming technique that uses portions of a computer document as a link to other documents. On a World Wide Web page, hypertext links can be a short string of words, a simulated on-screen button, or a picture.

hypothesis   In science, a possible explanation for a physical phenomenon that needs to be proven by experimentation.

icon   A small picture used to represent a computer program. When selected, an icon activates the application it represents.

immersion The sense of being totally surrounded by a virtual environment.

immersive Capable of creating a sense of immersion in a virtual environment through programming techniques and/or a system of effectors.

integrated circuit A complete electrical circuit—including wires, switches, and other components—that has been etched onto a single chip of material such as silicon.

interactive Capable of conducting command-and-response interactions between users and computers with little or no time lag. Also, virtual environments capable of responding immediately to any changes the user makes.

interaural amplitude difference The differing force with which sound waves hit each ear, depending on which ear is closer to the source of the sound waves.

interaural time difference The short delay between the moment sound waves reach one ear and the moment they reach the other.

Internet A globe-spanning network of interconnected computer systems. Though it is the most well-known network, the Internet is actually just one of several networks that exist to help people exchange news and ideas with one another.

joystick A post-shaped control device that allows movement in two of the three dimensions. A 3-D joystick allows movement in all three dimensions (forward/back, left/right, up/down).

lag time The delay between an action and the effects of that action. In VR, lag time reflects how long it takes a virtual environment to catch up to a user's movement.

LCD *See* LIQUID-CRYSTAL DISPLAY.

LED *See* LIGHT-EMITTING DIODE.

light-emitting diode (LED) A diode is an electronic component that lets current flow in one direction but prevents it from flowing in the other. A light-emitting diode is a diode that produces light as current flows through it. Unlike incandescent light bulbs, LEDs use very little energy.

liquid crystal A normally transparent liquid material that turns opaque when an electric current runs through it.

liquid-crystal display (LCD) A computer display made up of a liquid-crystal material trapped between separate layers of glass or plastic.

mechanical tracker A position tracker that uses electronic linkages attached to mechanical joints to measure movement.

microcomputer   *See* PERSONAL COMPUTER.

microprocessor   A type of integrated circuit that contains a computer's master control circuitry.

minicomputer   A table-size or cabinet-size computer that appeared in the early- to mid-1960s, following the introduction of TRANSISTORS to computer circuitry.

monoscopic   A visual display that presents a single, two-dimensional image.

motion tracker   *See* POSITION TRACKER.

mouse   A computer device that uses a rolling ball and at least one button to control an on-screen cursor. A standard computer mouse provides only two-dimensional (up/down and left/right) movement.

mouse, 3-D   A computer mouse used to navigate in three-dimensional computer environments.

nanometer   One-billionth of a meter, roughly 39 billionths (0.000000039) of an inch.

optical fiber   A solid, very thin glass or plastic fiber that can transmit light around curves.

PC   *See* PERSONAL COMPUTER.

persistence of vision   A phenomenon of human sight. The eyes and brain retain an image of an object for a split second after that object leaves a person's line of sight. This image retention explains why people can watch a movie—really just a rapid series of separate images—and perceive a continuous flow of action.

personal computer (PC)   A personal computer is designed to perform fairly simple tasks, such as organizing family finances, gaining access to the Internet, playing games, or managing the paperwork of a small office. PCs rely on a single central processing unit, supplemented by special-purpose processors, to perform the calculations that these tasks require. Because of their size, PCs are also known as microcomputers and desktop computers.

photoreceptor   A mechanical or electronic device, or a group of cells, that can detect light.

pixel   From "picture element." A small block of color used to create a computer graphic image.

polarity   The alignment of an electromagnetic force such as light waves. An example is the north-south orientation of a magnetic field.

polarization   The separation of an electromagnetic force into different polarities.

polarizer   Something that can separate polarities.

polyline   In computer graphics, a curved line that is created by connecting a series of line segments. Changing the angle of each line segment determines how and where the line curves.

position tracker   An effector that lets a VR system monitor which way a user moves his or her head, arms, legs, hands, or whole body. Position trackers can be magnetic, sonic, mechanical, or gyroscopic.

proprioception   The ability of the body to sense its own movement and position through special sensory cells in the muscles, joints, and inner ear.

proprioceptor   One of the special sensory cells the body uses to generate the cues of proprioception.

ray-tracing   A way to determine how objects in a virtual world would be illuminated by calculating the path light rays would take from the viewer's eye to the objects. In effect, this method involves pretending to make light waves "back up" from the eyes to the objects in a virtual environment.

reality simulator   A computer system specially designed to create and run VR simulations.

refresh rate   The number of times per second that a computer redraws the images it displays. VR systems need to maintain a refresh rate of 30 frames per second to create and maintain a sense of 3-D immersion.

render   To create a computer graphic image, in particular a three-dimensional image.

scanning probe microscope   A microscope that scans extremely small object by passing a needlelike probe over its surface.

scientific method   The process of explaining natural phenomena through observation, hypothesis, and experimentation. The scientific method also involves verification of one's work by other scientists.

semicircular canals   Three fluid-filled tubes that form part of the inner ear and that help the body maintain its balance. Each tube makes a half loop along one of the Cartesian axes.

semiconductor   A material that provides partial resistance to an electrical current flowing through itself.

semitransparent mirror   A reflecting surface that lets the viewer see a reflected image overlaid on the view of objects behind the mirror.

shutter glasses   A set of liquid-crystal lenses that rapidly flicker between transparency and opacity in sync with a rapidly alternating left-eye/right-eye computer display. This method gives a good simulation of three-dimensional sight.

six-degree-of-freedom (6DOF)   Allowing one to move along and spin around all three axes of the three-dimensional world.

sonic tracker   A position tracker that monitors movement using tiny microphones that pick up ultrasonic pulses from a fixed emitter.

sound waves   Disturbances in the air or other materials that humans can interpret as sound.

spatial sound   Sound as it is heard in the physical world.

spline   In computer graphics, a curved line whose curve is determined according to a mathematical equation.

spreadsheet   A computer accounting program that organizes financial data by placing it in categories in a series of columns and rows; also, a printed version of such a form.

stereophonic sound   Sound recorded with two or more microphones to give a more widespread effect.

stereoscopic vision   The visual perception of length, width, and depth.

supercomputer   A very fast and very powerful computer that is able to perform a great number of mathematical operations in a very short time. Supercomputers usually are the fastest and most expensive computers available at any given time.

tactile feedback   An effector that mimics physical sensations (such as how a brick wall feels) by stimulating the touch receptors in the skin. Inflatable air sacs or vibrating panels in a wired glove are some examples of tactile feedback.

teleoperation   A technique of using virtual-reality displays to operate remotely controlled robots or other machinery.

telepresence   *See* TELEOPERATION.

telerobotics   *See* TELEOPERATION.

texture map   A computer image, such as a photo of a textured surface, that can be pasted over a virtual object.

three-degree-of-freedom (3DOF)   Allowing one to move along the three axes of the three-dimensional world but not to spin around them.

three-dimensional mouse (3-D mouse)   *See* MOUSE, 3-D.

transducer   Any device or material that converts one form of energy to another. For example, a radio speaker, which takes electrical impulses and converts them to sound waves, is a form of transducer.

transistor   An electronic component based around a semiconductor that can be used as a switch in an electric circuit.

ultrasonic   A sound wave with a higher frequency than that which humans can hear.

vacuum tube   A closed glass tube from which all air has been removed and which contains one or more electric wires. Vacuum tubes were used as switches in many early computers.

VCASS   *See* VISUALLY COUPLED AIRBORNE SYSTEMS SIMULATOR.

VET   *See* VIRTUAL ENVIRONMENT TECHNOLOGY.

VIEW   *See* VIRTUAL IMMERSIVE ENVIRONMENT WORKSTATION.

virtual   The word itself means something that exists in theory or in the imagination but not in fact. Since the late 1970s, *virtual* also has come to mean just about anything that exists as a computer file or that can be accomplished using computer networks.

virtual architecture   This term has two general meanings. It can refer to a combination of computer hardware and software, including virtual reality that is used to design buildings. It also can refer to a three-dimensional construct that mimics the function of a real-world building but exists only in a virtual environment.

virtual environment   A three-dimensional, immersive, interactive world designed for use in virtual reality.

virtual environment technology (VET)   Another term for virtual reality.

virtual heritage   The use of virtual reality and other computer-graphics techniques to create digital models of historic buildings, ancient settlements, and other relics of past cultures and civilizations. The term includes alterations to these models that show how the original structures may have looked when new.

Virtual Immersive Environment Workstation (VIEW)   A project of the NASA Ames Research Center that was the first fully functional goggle-and-glove virtual-reality system in the world. It was an expansion of the earlier Virtual Visual Environment Display.

virtual presence   Another term for virtual reality.

virtual reality   A form of computer technology that creates the effect of immersing its user in a three-dimensional, computer-generated artificial world.

Virtual Reality Modeling Language (VRML)   A form of programming language that allows programmers to create three-dimensional environments that can be transmitted over the World Wide Web.

Virtual Visual Environment Display (VIVED)   A project of the NASA Ames Research Center that created the first successful low-budget 3-D visual display.

visual tracker   A position tracker that uses video cameras to monitor where and how users move in a physical space. Some institutions are working on visual tracker systems in which the users wear the cameras and the cameras gauge movement by tracing ceiling-mounted LEDs.

Visually Coupled Airborne Systems Simulator (VCASS)   An experimental jet fighter HMD system that displayed flight information, air and ground targets, and terrain features as an easily comprehended virtual environment.

VIVED   *See* VIRTUAL VISUAL ENVIRONMENT DISPLAY.

VR   *See* VIRTUAL REALITY.

VRML   *See* VIRTUAL REALITY MODELING LANGUAGE.

wand   An effector that acts much like a 3-D mouse but is shaped like a television remote control or a joystick without a base. Most wands house a magnetic or gyroscopic position *tracker.*

wave   A pulse of energy that travels along or through something. There are two types of waves. *Transverse* waves, such as ocean waves, cause vibrations that are perpendicular to their path of movement. *Longitudinal* or *compression* waves, such as sound waves, cause vibrations that are parallel to their path of movement.

wired glove   A glove-shaped effector that monitors the position of a user's hand and how far the user's fingers bend. Most wired gloves incorporate optical fibers to measure finger flex and have one or more position trackers, usually magnetic. Some wired gloves are rigged to provide tactile feedback.

World Wide Web (WWW)   This is a subset of the Internet that presents information in a form that mimics pages from magazines or advertising brochures. Web pages can be connected via hyperlinks.

WWW   *See* WORLD WIDE WEB.

workstation   A very fast, very powerful personal computer designed specifically for advanced computer graphics or other projects that involve intensive calculations.

FURTHER READING

"Activeworlds to Cultivate New, Innovative Virtual Research Lab for Future Harvest Centers." Found on-line at Yahoo!Finance, March 13, 2001.

"Air Typing into a PDA." Forbes.com, November 19, 2001. Available on-line. URL: http://www.forbes.com/2001/11/19/1119tentech.html.

"A Virtual World Is Taking Shape in Research Labs." *Los Angeles Times*, Monday, February 5, 2001. Available on-line. URL: http://www.latimes.com/business/20010205/t000010695.html.

Anders, Peter. *Envisioning Cyberspace: Designing 3D Electronic Spaces.* New York: McGraw-Hill, 1999.

Baum, David. "Assets in Wonderland." *Byte* July 1995: 111–117.

Beier, K.-P. "Virtual Reality: A Short Introduction." Available on-line. URL: http://www-vrl.umich.edu/intro/index.html.

Bertol, Daniela, and David Foell. *Designing Digital Spaces: An Architect's Guide to Virtual Reality.* New York: Wiley & Sons, 1997.

"BP Amoco Donates Lab to University of Colorado." Found on-line through Reuters news wire/Yahoo! News, Wednesday, October 18, 2001. Similar article available on-line. URL: http://www.colorado.edu/engineering/cue01/research/bp.html

Brooks, Frederick P., Jr. "Special Report: What's Real about Virtual Reality?" *IEEE Computer Graphics & Applications* Vol. 20, No. 6 (November/December 1999): 16–27.

Calverly, Bob. "Next-Generation War Games." *USC Trojan Family Magazine* Vol. 34, No. 1 (Spring 2002): 34–39.

Campbell-Kelly, Martin, and William Aspray. *Computer: A History of the Information Machine.* New York: Basic Books, 1996.

Carnoy, David. "Life in the Fast Lane: A Guide to the Internet's Best Broadband Destinations." *Fortune* Vol. 142, No. 8 (October 9, 2000): 308.

Ceruzzi, Paul E. *A History of Modern Computing.* Cambridge, Mass.: The MIT Press, 1998.

Chapman, Paul, and others. "Real-Time Visualization in the Offshore Industry." *IEEE Computer Graphics & Applications* Vol. 21, No. 4 (July/August 2001): 6–10.

Chen, Chaomei. *Information Visualization and Virtual Environments*. London: Springer-Verlag London Limited, 1999.

Chinnock, Chris. "Virtual Reality Goes to Work." *Byte*, March 1996, 26–27.

Daviss, Bennett. "Grand Illusions." *Discover* Vol. 11, No. 6 (June 1990): 36–41.

Delaney, Ben. "Moving to the Mainstream." *Computer Graphics World* Vol. 24, No. 10 (October 2001).

———. "Virtual Course, Real Sweat." *Computer Graphics World* Vol. 24, No. 7 (July 2001): 48–52.

Ditlea, Steve. "Tomorrow's Teleconferencing." *Computer Graphics World* Vol. 24, No. 1 (January 2001): 36–40.

"Doctors in New York Use Robot to Operate in France." Found on-line through Reuters news wire/Yahoo! News, Wednesday, September 18, 2001. Available on-line. URL: http://www.spectrum.ieee.org/news/cache/ReutersOnlineScience/09_19_2001. romta0815-story-bcscience-healthrobotdc.html

"Doctors Warn of Gaming's Health Risks." Reuters news wire/CNET News.com, February 1, 2002. Available on-line. URL: http://news.com.com/2100-1040-827666.html.

Doyle, Audrey. "Pioneering Prototypes." *Computer Graphics World* Vol. 23, No. 9 (September 2000): 39–47.

Draper, Mark H. "Can Your Eyes Make You Sick?: Investigating the Relationship between the Vestibulo-ocular Reflex and Virtual Reality" (Paper, Human Interface Technology Laboratory, University of Washington, 1996). Available on-line. URL: http://www.hitl.washington.edu/publications/r-96-3/.

Eddings, Joshua. *How Virtual Reality Works*. Emeryville, Calif.: Ziff-Davis Press, 1994.

"Focus: Panoramic technology." *CGI* Vol. 6, No. 4: 38–41.

"For Your Eyes Only" (Personal Technology), *Fortune* Vol. 143, No. 5 (March 5, 2001): 242.

Furness, Dr. Thomas. Telephone interview with the author. Tuesday, October 24, 2001.

Gottschalk, Mark A., and Sharon Machlis. "Engineering Enters the Virtual World." *Design News* November 7, 1994: 52–63.

Halfhill, Tom R. "See You Around." *Byte* May 1995: 85–90.

Hanson, Mary. "Something to Smile About: 3D Graphics Are Revolutionizing Oral Health Care." *IEEE Computer Graphics and Applications* Vol. 21, No. 4 (July/August 2001): 14–20.

Hartwig, Glenn. "Better Mousetrap Bites Dog." *Desktop Engineering* July 2001: 36–45.

Heft, Miguel. "Augmented Reality Scientists Want Respect." *Wired News* June 2, 1997. Available on-line. URL: http://www.wired.com//news/technology/0,1282,4179,00.html.

Heudin, Jean-Claude, ed. *Virtual Worlds: Synthetic Universes, Digital Life, and Complexity*. Reading, Mass.: Perseus Books, 1999.

Hodges, Mark. "Cyber Therapy." *Computer Graphics World* Vol. 24, No. 1 (January 2001): 28–34.

"Home of Golf Offers Virtual Reality Preparation." Found on-line through Reuters news wire/Yahoo! News, Monday, October 15, 2001. Related press release available on-line. URL: http://www.standrews.org.uk/news/pr/pr2001/press30.htm

Jacqué, Dave. "Making Virtual Reality a Reality." *Logos* Vol. 17, No. 1 (Spring 1999). Available on-line. URL: http://www.logos.com.

Johnson, R. Colin. "Lab Probes Long-term Effects of Exposure to Virtual Reality." EE Times, February 2, 1999. Available on-line. URL: http://www.eet.com/story/OEG19990202S0055.

Johnson, Susan Court. "As the Virtual World Turns." *California Computer News*, December 1999. Available on-line. URL: http://www.ccnmag.com/Dec99/ActiveWorlds.htm.

Konrad, Rachel. "Logitech Gets Touchy-Feely with New Mouse." CNET News.Com, Friday, August 18, 2000. Available on-line. URL: http://news.cnet.com/news/0-1006-200-2555759.html.

———. "Researchers Tout Touchy-Feely Technology." CNET News.Com, Friday, September 7, 2001. Available on-line: URL: http://news.cnet.com/news/0-1007-200-7069493.html.

Laiserin, Jerry. "Places in Time." *Computer Graphics World* Vol. 23, No. 11 (November 2000): 40–44.

Mahoney, Diana Phillips. "Graphics on the Internet." Part 3: Tomorrow's Internet. *Computer Graphics World* Vol. 23, No. 12 (December 2000): 45–49.

———. "Seeing Sound." *Computer Graphics World* Vol. 24, No. 8 (August 2001): 35–42.

"Marines Use 'Virtual Reality' for Missile Training." Found on-line through Reuters news wire/Yahoo! News, Wednesday, October 31, 2001.

Masson, Terrence. *CG 101: A Computer Graphics Industry Reference.* Indianapolis, Ind.: New Riders Publishing, 1999.

Möller, Tomas, and Eric Haines. *Real-Time Rendering.* Natick, Mass.: A. K. Peters, 1999.

Moltenbrey, Karen. "Hull Raising (Engineers Simulate the Recovery of the Disabled Russian Submarine *Kursk*)." *Computer Graphics World* Vol. 24, No. 7 (July 2001): 25–29.

———. "No Bones about It." *Computer Graphics World* Vol. 24, No. 2 (February 2001): 24–30.

———. "Preserving the Past." *Computer Graphics World* Vol. 24, No. 9 (September 2001): 24–30.

———. "Tornado Watchers." *Computer Graphics World* Vol. 23, No. 9 (September 2000): 24–28.

Moody, Fred. *The Visionary Position: The Inside Story of the Digital Dreamers Who Are Making Virtual Reality a Reality.* New York: Times Business, 1999.

"The nanoManipulator: A Virtual-Reality Interface to Scanned-Probe Microscopes." Available on-line. URL: http://www.cs.unc.edu/Research/nano.

Neumann, Dr. Ulrich. Interview with author at University of Southern California's Integrated Media Systems Center. Friday, August 17, 2001.

Neumann, Ulrich, and Suya You. "Tracking for Augmented Reality." Available on-line. URL: http://imsc.usc.edu.

Neumann, Ulrich, Anand Srinivasan, and Thomas Pintaric. "PiV: Panoramic Immersivision." Available on-line. URL: http://imsc.usc.edu.

Newman, Kevin. "Point, Click . . . and Touch?" ABCNEWS.com, October 16, 2000. Available on-line. URL: http://www.abcnews.com.

Nikias, Max. "Immersive Environments." *Zone News*, January 2000: 89–92.

"Ohio Surgeons Test Goggles." Found on-line through Associated Press news wire/Yahoo! News, Sunday, February 27, 2000.

On Technology. "Don't Just Watch TV, Wear It." ABCNEWS.com, 1999. Available on-line. URL: http://abcnews.go.com/sections/tech/FredMoody/moody18.html.

Overton, Rick. "Fax It Up, Scotty: 3D Printing Turns the Humble Inkjet Printer into a Foundry for Everything from Rocket Nozzles to Hip Bones." *Business 2.0* March 6, 2001. Available on-line. URL: http://www.business2.com/content/channels/technology/2001/02/26/26857.

Packer, Randall, and Ken Jordan, eds. *Multimedia: From Wagner to Virtual Reality*. New York: W. W. Norton & Co., 2001.

Papka, Michael E., Rick Stevens, and Matthew Szymanski. "Collaborative Virtual Reality Environments for Computational Science and Design." In *Computer-Aided Design of High-Temperature Materials*, Topics in Physical Chemistry series, edited by Alexander Pechenik, Rajiv K. Kalia, and Priya Vashishta, 410–421. New York: Oxford University Press, 1999.

Perkins, Sid. "A Makeover for an Old Friend." *Science News* Vol. 158, No. 19 (November 4, 2000): 300–302.

Pimentel, Ken, and Kevin Teixeira. *Virtual Reality: Through the New Looking Glass*, 2nd edition. New York: McGraw-Hill, 1995.

Potter, Caren D. "Ford, BMW, and Boeing Reap Real Rewards from Virtual Factories." *Computer Graphics World* Vol. 23, No. 2 (February 2000). Available on-line: www.cgw.com.

Pountain, Dick. "VR Meets Reality." *Byte* July 1996: 93–98.

Rheingold, Howard. *The Virtual Community: Homesteading on the Electronic Frontier (revised edition)*. Cambridge, Mass.: The MIT Press, 2000.

———. *Virtual Reality*. New York: Simon & Schuster, 1991.

Robertson, Barbara. "Artists Use Caves and Other VR Displays to Explore Interactive Environments." *Computer Graphics World* Vol. 24, No. 11 (November 2001). Available on-line. URL: www.cgw.com.

"Robots Help Long-Distance Surgery." Found on-line from AP Health-Science news wire at www.newsday.com, November 5, 2000. Similar article available on-line. URL: http://www.jsonline.com/alive/ap/nov00/ap-exp-telemedicin110500.asp.

Scott, David. "Virtual Tours Assist Home Hunters with Initial Search." *Reno (Nev.) Gazette-Journal*, Friday, June 9, 2000, sec. D.

"Shuttle Discovery Astronauts to Simulate Disasters." Found on-line through Reuters news wire/Yahoo! News, Wednesday, October 18, 2000. Similar article available on-line. URL: http://www.abc.net.au/science/news/stories/s201451.htm

"Singapore Has Scientific Ambitions." AP International news wire, April 14, 2001. Found on-line through www.newsday.com.

Singhal, Sandeep, and Michael Zyda. *Networked Virtual Environments: Design and Implementation*. New York: ACM Press, 1999.

Stanney, Kay M., Ronald R. Mourant, and Robert S. Kennedy. "Human Factors Issues in Virtual Environments: A Review of the Literature." *Presence* Vol. 7, No. 4 (August 1998): 327–351.

"Steering Molecules by Feel." *NASnews* Vol. 4, No. 2 (March-April 1999). Available on-line. URL: http://nas.nasa.gov/Pubs/NASnews/1999/03/index.html.

"Superscape Delivers Interactive 3D for Safety Training at Ford." Available on-line. URL: http://www.superscape.com/company/pressroom.asp.

"Superscape Works with Ford on Interactive 3D Safety Training." The Auto Channel, April 3, 2001. Available on-line. URL: http://www.theautochannel.com/news/2001/04/03/017892.html.

Technofile, *T3: Tomorrow's Technology Today* No. 38 (October 1999): 26.

Technology Review. *VR News.* Available on-line. URL: http://www.vrnews.com. "The CEJ DOA (Dictionary of Acronyms." Available on-line. URL: http://www.cyberedge.com/4a6.html.

U.S. Congress, Office of Technology Assessment, *Virtual Reality and Technologies for Combat Simulation—Background Paper,* OTA-BP-ISS-136 (Washington, D.C.: U.S. Government Printing Office, September 1994).

Vinzant, Carol. "Kapow! Zap! Gizmos Give Superhero Powers." *Fortune* Vol. 142, No. 1 (July 10, 2000): 64.

"Virtual Environments for Shipboard Damage Control and Firefighting Research." Available on-line. URL: http://www.chemistry.nrl.navy.mil/damagecontrol/vr.html.

"Virtual Hurricanes: Computer Model Pushes the Frontier." Reprinted from *ScienceDaily Magazine*, Friday, August 3, 2001. Available on-line. URL: http://www.sciencedaily.com/releases/2001/08/010803083644.htm.

"The Virtual Lexicon: a Glossary of VR Terms." Available on-line. URL: http://www.cyberedge.com/4al.html.

"Virtual Reality Frees Some from Their Phobias." CNN.com, June 21, 2000. Available on-line. URL: http://www.cnn.com/2000/US/06/21/virtual.phobias/.

"Virtual Reality Helps Astronauts Adapt to Space." Cosmiverse.com, July 11, 2001. Available on-line. URL: http://www.cosmiverse.com/space07110105.html.

"Virtual Reality Images Allow 'Fantastic Voyage' Tour of the Body." Radiological Society of North America, November 28, 2000. Available on-line. URL: http://www.rsna.org or http://www.radiologyinfo.org.

"Virtual Reality Training Tool Pits Emergency Rescue Teams Against Computerized Terrorist Attack." (News release). Available on-line. URL: http://www.sandia.gov.

"Virtual Therapy Tames Terrors." *USA Weekend* September 29-October 1, 2000: 9.

Weishar, Peter. *Digital Space: Designing Virtual Environments.* New York: McGraw-Hill, 1998.

Wen, Howard. "Sim Dizzy: Does Half-Life Make You Sick? Well, You're Not Alone. Plenty of Gamers Suffer from Simulation Sickness." Salon.com magazine, August 11, 2000. Available on-line. URL: http://www.salon.com.

WORLD WIDE WEB SITES

The following list of sites on the World Wide Web represents just a small sample of the universities, organizations, and corporations that are connected with virtual reality. However, these sites will serve as good starting points for up-to-date information on virtual reality and its uses. The addresses for the sites were current as of January 2002; owing to the nature of the Internet and the rapid changes that can take place there, however, they may have changed after this book was published. If so, and if the site has not gone out of business, the new addresses might be found by searching the Web for the site's name. Otherwise, running a search for the terms *virtual reality, virtual environment,* or *immersive computing* should yield enough information to satisfy anyone's curiosity.

Academic Sites

1. Department of Computer Science, University of North Carolina at Chapel Hill, Chapel Hill, N.C.: http://www.cs.unc.edu
2. Electronic Visualization Laboratory, University of Illinois at Chicago, Chicago, Ill.: http://www.evl.uic.edu
3. Human Interface Technology Laboratory, University of Washington, Seattle, Wash.: http://www.hitl.washington.edu
4. Immersive Media Systems Center, University of Southern California, Los Angeles, Calif.: http://www.imsc.usc.edu
5. MIT Media Lab, Massachusetts Institute of Technology, Cambridge, Mass.: http://www.media.met.edu

6. Virtual Reality and Education Laboratory, East Carolina University, Greenville, N.C.: http://www.soe.ecu.edu/vr/vrel.htm
7. Virtual Reality Laboratory, University of Michigan, Ann Arbor, Mich.: http://www-VRL.umich.edu
8. VLearn 3D, a site that provides information and links to three-dimensional educational sites: http://www.vlearn3d.org

General Information Sites

1. Association for Computing Machinery, a professional organization for computer researchers that supports a number of graphics and immersive computing technology special interest groups, or SIGs: http://www.acm.org (The ACM's Special Interest Group for Graphics—SIGGRAPH—sponsors one of the world's biggest computer conferences each year, at which virtual-reality projects and products are prominently featured.)
2. IEEE Computer Society, a professional organization for computer researchers organized under the Institute of Electric and Electronic Engineers: http://www.computer.org
3. VR News, a website devoted to the latest information on virtual reality and other computing applications: http://www.vrnews.com
4. The VR Source, an information and sales site: http://www.vrsource.org
5. Virtual Medical Worlds Magazine, an on-line magazine that focuses on medical uses of virtual reality and other multimedia computing technologies: http://www.hoise.com/vmw
6. CGW.com, the on-line version of *Computer Graphic World* magazine, which features articles on graphics applications including VR, film and television animation, computer-aided design, and multimedia: http://www.cgw.com

Virtual Reality Company Sites

1. Activeworlds Inc., a company that makes three-dimensional browser software for the World Wide Web and hosts a range of interactive on-line communities: http://www.activeworlds.com
2. Fakespace Systems Inc., one of the oldest firms involved in building and selling immersive environment systems: http://www.fakespace.com

3. SensAble Technologies Inc., the company that manufacturers the PHANTOM haptic manipulation and design tool, as well as software tools for simulating tactile sensations: http://www.sensable.com

4. 5DT, Inc. (Fifth Dimension Technologies), a manufacturer of virtual-reality effectors and virtual environments: http://www.5dt.com

5. I-O Display Systems, a manufacturer of monoscopic and stereoscopic head-mounted eyeglass and visor-style displays: http://www.i-glasses.com

6. Immersion Corporation, a company that makes and licenses designs for tactile effectors and software: http://www.immersion.com

7. Learning Sites Inc., one of a number of companies involved in virtual archaeological reconstructions: http://www.learningsites.com

8. Sense8, a company that produces three-dimensional software creation programs: http://www.sense8.com

9. SGI (Silicon Graphics Inc.), one of the oldest companies that manufactures computers and displays for many applications, including immersive computing environments: http://www.sgi.com

10. Virtual Presence, a British company that makes virtual-reality products and environments: http://www.vrweb.com

INDEX

Italic page numbers indicate illustrations.